MW01120116

Praise for *MDM for Customer Data*

"Kelvin has conveyed his deep understanding of the business value and technol
ogy that motivates organizations to become customer centric. The explanations
in this book are based on the reality that every organization has a different start
ing point in the journey to become customer centric. Kelvin provides practical
advice on the different styles of implementation and the advantages and disad
vantages of each approach. He also provides real life examples of organizations
that have implemented solutions and how they achieved business benefits. This
book is a must have for anyone who has been given the opportunity to make their
organization more customer centric."

DOUGLAS P. THOMPSON
Senior Enterprise Architect, Enterprise Customer, SunTrust Bank

"In today's competitive climate, being customer centric is no longer a business
strategy that differentiates one company from another. However, it is still a difficult goal for many to achieve. Those who succeed can offer a differentiating customer experience that is truly unique and inspires loyalty and lasting
relationships. This book offers a practical approach to selecting an architecture
and roadmap that supports such a strategy. Kelvin offers case studies from many
years of experience in implementations across many large financial institutions
and other industries. Each company can have a different approach towards the
target state. If you need to understand how to select the best option for your com
pany, he offers guidelines for selecting the architecture options and identifies the
associated benefits of each."

CHAI LAM
Managing Enterprise Architect, Bank of Montreal Financial Group

MDM
for Customer Data

MDM
for Customer Data

Optimizing Customer Centric
Management of Your Business

Kelvin K. A. Looi

MC Press Online, LP

Lewisville, TX 75077

MDM for Customer Data: Optimizing Customer Centric Management of Your Business
Kelvin K.A. Looi

First Printing—October 2009

Every attempt has been made to provide correct information. However, the publisher and the author do not guarantee the accuracy of the book and do not assume responsibility for information in cluded in or omitted from it.

IBM is a trademark of International Business Machines Corporation in the United States, other countries, or both. All other product names are trademarked or copyrighted by their respective manufacturers.

MC Press offers excellent discounts on this book when ordered in quantity for bulk purchases or special sales, which may include custom covers and content particular to your business, training goals, marketing
focus, and branding interest.

For information regarding permissions or special orders, please contact:
MC Press
Corporate Offices
125 N. Woodland Trail
Lewisville, TX 75077 USA

For information regarding sales and/or customer service, please contact:
MC Press
P.O. Box 4300
Big Sandy, TX 75755-4300 USA

ISBN: 978-158347-350-4

Acknowledgements

The inspiration to write this book came from my ten-year involvement helping organizations globally understand and use MDM technology solution to enable their business operation to be more customer-centric. This book was written during many hours on planes and in hotels while visiting organizations around the world. This book would not have happened without the encouragement and support from my family—my wife Jane and my two daughters Jennifer and Michelle. Special thanks also go to Jennifer who found time away from her heavy school work, and May Li, my colleague, who helped me proof read and edit the book. I would also like to thank Susan Visser and my boss, Kevin Painter, who helped to push this book to completion. Last, but not least are the founders, leaders, and co-workers of DWL (acquired by IBM), the company that made *MDM for Customer Data* a reality and pioneered many MDM implementations throughout the world. Special mentions from DWL include Justin LaFayette, Al Digout, John Baumstark, Simon Chong, and Bruce McPherson. All of these people, in one way or another, guided me and allowed me the opportunities to enrich my knowledge on MDM.

September 2009

Contents

Introduction

"Customer-centric" operations are the objective of many organizations. These organizations have promised their boards and shareholders, have received buy-in from their employees, and have told their customers that "customer-centric" operations are the wave of the future. This same customer-centric objective has formed a common strategic theme across all industries—banks, insurance companies, health care organizations, manufacturing sectors, airlines, telecommunications companies, and consumer package goods businesses—and even in the public sector.

Organizations have invested a lot of money over a long time in new technology that will enable them to achieve this promised customer-centric objective. Projects with names such as Single Customer View, Common Customer View, Customer Operational Data Store (ODS), Client Information File (CIF), Single View of Citizen, and many others have been promoted in many companies as solutions to customer-centric processing issues. Unfortunately, not many of these projects have succeeded. So, how do organizations measure themselves to be successful at being customer-centric? What exactly does it means to be customer-centric?

Customer Relationship Management (CRM) and data warehouse solutions are a few examples of technologies that have tried to provide the panacea of customer-centricity, but have fallen short of the goal. Why aren't CRM and data warehouses as effective in enabling customer-centric operations as they're hyped to be? Why is being customer-centric so difficult? What goes wrong? And, more importantly, what is the solution?

The Customer MDM Solution

A software solution called Master Data Management (MDM) just may be the "cure-all" that organizations can implement to achieve customer-centricity. The MDM solution can be used for a multitude of data domains, such as customer, product, account, and more. This solution to managing the customer data domain is also known in the industry as the Customer Data Integration (CDI) solution. For simplicity, we will call this concept the Customer MDM solution. So, is the Customer MDM solution the missing link to enabling a customer-centric organization?

If the MDM solution is the key, what else is needed? How can existing and new customer data enter this solution? What do you do with the customer data that currently exist in your various business systems? Do you get rid of the other systems, or do you synchronize the changes?

Once you are convinced that MDM is the way to go, where and how do you start to implement it? Do you do this using a "big bang" approach, or in phases? What are your options? How do organizations justify this approach to customer-centricity, and where is the payback?

Customer MDM sounds a lot like the Client Information File (CIF) solution that exists in many organizations—especially in the big financial services companies. What can this Customer MDM solution provide that CIF cannot?

To be an organization with a truly customer-centric operation is not easy, because no one-size-fits-all solution exists. The Customer MDM solution seems to be the answer. But is it? This book may not be able to provide all the answers to implementing a solution to meet your organization's customer-centric operation objective, but it will certainly provide you with some viable answers to these important questions. Hopefully, with better insights into this new breed of MDM, you can make more informed decisions when implementing your own solution.

Chapter 1

The Elusive
Customer-centric Operation

Organizations have been trying to achieve a Single Customer View and provide customer-centric sales and services for a long time. How do you know when your organization is "customer-centric"? What exactly does it mean?

Defining "Customer-centric"

It is hard to universally define what it is to be customer-centric, primarily be cause of the difficulty inherent in the word "customer." *Customer* means differ ent things to different organizations: the retail operations of a bank may consider the individual account holder as its customer; a property and casualty insurance company may consider both the insured and claimants as its customers; a life in surance company may consider the agent who sells the company's insurance as its customer; a health care company may consider the doctor and pharmacist as its customers, a manufacturing company may consider both buyer and supplier as its customers; a government agency may consider all citizens as its customers. For simplicity, instead of citing examples using many different industries, the re tail banking and insurance industries will be used throughout this book as the predominant examples, since much of the population have bank accounts and in surance policies, thus making them easy to relate to. Hopefully, after reading this book you will gain a new understanding of Master Data Management (MDM) and be able to relate it back to your own industry and situation.

A good way to define a customer-centric operation is to view it from the customer's perspective—what they want to buy and how they wish to be served—not from the organization's perspective—how the organization wants to sell and service its customers. A distinction must be made about whether a customer is new (i.e., has no current or previous relationship with the organization) or already exists. For the sake of this definition, we will look at the customer-centric definition from an existing customer's perspective. New customers will offer the organization some slack when not being served in a customer-centric way, since the assumption is that the organization doesn't know who they are. Of course, the new customer still expects the organization to provide service with pleasantry and respect. However, once customer data is captured from the first instance of a business transaction, the customer's expectations will be higher. No excuses exist for the organization not to be customer-centric when providing further sales and services to this customer. A customer can be a person (e.g., for a retail bank) or even another organization (e.g., a customer of a corporate bank or supplier of a manufacturing company), but they all want the same things. They simply wish for the company to:

- Know who they are

- Know who they are related to (for a single customer, these relationships could be family household members, where they work, and related third parties that are of interest, such as their accountant, lawyer, etc. For an organization, relationships could include the organizational hierarchy, departments, employees, and related third parties that are of interest, such as any registered regulatory bodies, marketing associations, etc.)

- Know what products and/or services they own and/or subscribe to

- Know what products and/or services the rest of their family/business owns and/or subscribes to

- Know who they work for, in what capacity, and what their employers own

- Know their past interactions across all channels

- Know what new products are important to them

- Know when, where, and how to reach them (e.g., address, phone number, fax, e-mail, etc.) as well as when to use these channels and for what purpose

- Know their privacy preferences (whether they want to receive sales campaigns or not. If yes, for what products, through what channels and when) and protect their data against unwarranted access or usage

- Be up to date with information (e.g., when customers move or change phone numbers, they only want to have to notify the company once, not five times because they purchase five products)

- Provide consistent sales and service experiences across all channels

- Tell them about things that might be of interest without them having to ask

The list can go on and on, based on scenarios for different types of customers and lines of business (LOBs). But to keep things simple, we can summarize a customer-centric operation according to the following four "KEEP" categories:

- Knowledge (K):
  - Who they are
  - What products and/or services they have
  - Their interactions across all channels
  - How they want to be served and sold to across all channels

- Efficiency (E)
  - Requests should only need to be made once
  - Requests should be executed quickly and accurately

- Effectiveness (E)
  - Know how profitable they are or are not and treat them appropriately
  - Provide them consistent treatment across all channels

- Proactivity (P)
  - Predict what they need and tell them before they need it
  - Remind them of actions your company needs to do

The "Driving Test"

Let's use our regular banking experience as an example. I call this the "driving test" to see whether a bank is customer-centric in the way it interacts with me. Here's how the scenario works:

Let's start with my bank profile. I have a few accounts with my bank—a personal savings account, a personal checking account, a personal credit card with which I have joint ownership with my wife, and a brokerage account to manage my investments; I also have a company savings/checking account for the small business that I own and run from my home (called ABC Corporation), another credit card for my business, and a trust account for which my two daughters are the beneficiaries. I don't have much money in my personal savings and checking accounts as my money is invested and managed via the brokerage account and ABC Corporation.

My business has been reasonably successful, and I have just moved to a new and bigger home. In addition, I have installed a few new phone lines for my personal and business use.

I signed on to the bank Internet service and started to change my personal profile for my accounts. I managed to change my phone profile and then realized that I didn't have time to complete my address change, because I had to drive to an important customer meeting. So, I got into my car, put on my hands-free mobile phone device, called my bank's service number, and started to drive. Since I don't carry all my banking details with me, the number I dialed was the one listed on the back of my personal credit card in my wallet. So, here's where my "driving test" starts. I want to be able to do all my address change transactions for all my accounts with my bank during this drive, without having to have my hands off the steering wheel. If my bank can do this, it would have a pretty decent customer-centric operation and pass the test. Here are my expectations for what the customer service representative (CSR) knows and can do for me during this call:

- Knowledge of who I am. When the CSR picks up my call, he or she should already know my personal profile, my family members, my company, and all my accounts:
    - ➢ Most banks would have a technology solution to partially handle this. Telephone-to-computer technology would be available in most Interactive Voice Response (IVR) systems and call center CRM systems. If I don't disable my mobile phone number from being displayed at the other end, the current technology available in the call center should be able to use my phone number and inquire through available systems to figure out who I am. Most CRM systems would do a pretty decent job of managing my relationship profiles. However, knowing my total account portfolio is where these systems start to

have difficulty. Most IVR/CRM implementations are designed to handle certain product lines. The most likely case is that the CSR from the call center that I dialed using the telephone number listed on the back of my credit card will know my credit card's portfolio, but not the rest of my accounts. Some banks may consolidate the call center services of all the businesses within their retail bank operation. This will improve their knowledge of the customer profile across retail banking. However, information from other LOBs, such as investment and corporate banking, for the same customer will be missing.

- Authenticate me to make sure I am really who I say I am. Anybody could have picked up my mobile and called. The CSR should ask me a few questions that only I would know the answers to in order to authenticate me:

  ➤ Note here that I said my hands must always be on the steering wheel: I can't reach into my wallet and pull out my credit card. The CSR cannot insist on my knowledge of my credit card number before we can proceed. I should not be expected to remember my credit card number (until this day, I do not). This is where many organizations fail the driving test. Many will still require you to state your account number or product number before you can proceed any further—thus marking them as a very account- or product-centric operation.

- Know that I changed my phone number on the Internet a few minutes ago and can verify that the changes went through correctly for all my accounts:

  ➤ The CSR should know my interaction history. This is another weak point for most organizations. Some of those with CRM technology can handle interaction history, but only if you are using the same channel. That is, if I called the call center channel a few minutes ago, and then again now, the bank would know. But, since I did my earlier transactions through the web channel, this is not captured, at least not in real time. Some CRM implementations might load the interaction history from the web channels, but this typically happens in batch mode (normally overnight). As we all know, this is a real-time world. Any delay in the propagation of information is going to negatively affect your customer service or sales. For those of you who are not familiar with information technology terminology, *batch processing* a way to accumulate all the changes made to a database over a period of time. These changes are then submitted for processing to the system all at the same time, in batches, when the system is less busy, typically after business hours.

> To make matters worse, many organizations have multiple CRM instances, one for each product line, because that's how most CRM software is designed. Using our banking example again, in any typical bank, a separate CRM implementation instance is used for credit cards, retail banking, investment banking, commercial banking, etc. Most, if not all, CRM vendors have done a bad job in synchronizing and sharing information across all CRM applications. This gets worse when you start to use different CRM solutions from different vendors for different LOBs. Some organizations try to implement one instance of the CRM solution (note that I mention one instance, not multiple instances of the same solution) as the panacea. This strategy is not bad from a cost-cutting perspective, but it is very difficult to do. If your organization is a small, simple, one-line business, then it might be achievable. But the bigger and more diverse your business, the more challenging it's going to be to consolidate all your CSR channels to use one instance of a CRM solution. It gets worse in this day and age of mergers and acquisitions. When your organization merges, acquires, or gets acquired by another organization, you have to do this all over again.

> Some people will argue that data warehouse technology can handle interaction history across all channels. There is some truth to this, but it is manageable only in batch mode, not in real time. Some data warehouse diehards will try to turn their data warehouse into a real-time system or an operational data warehouse system. As much as we'd all love to be able to turn a batch analytical processing system into a real-time operating system, this is not efficient. Most operational warehouses are used to enable real-time access to the final analytical results, not to any of the base data.

- Efficiently handle the address change for me and all my accounts:
  > Here is where the operational aspect of this call starts to kick in. It's no longer about knowing and viewing, it's about adding and changing. This is where the rubber hits the road in a customer-centric operation, the ability to do "once-and-done" processing. That's why I don't like the world "view" in "single customer view" projects. Many business users have told their IT department to provide a "single customer view" solution, and a lot of times, that's what they get—a solution that might support the single customer *view* process but not the single

customer *change* process. In many cases, since no single update capability is available, the view is accomplished by consolidating customer information from many source systems. This inherently forces a lot of consolidation to be done via batch processes and therefore provides an out-of-date view. So, be careful what you ask for when you want a "single customer view" project. One of my former bosses once said to me: "Be careful what you ask for, you just might get it." This time-honored warning holds equally true in developing customer-centric solutions.

  - ➢ Statistics might vary based on location, but I am told that as many as one out of every 20 Americans changes his or her address every year. Of course, your customers may differ based on the nature of the product you sell and the location you operate in. However, based on the real-estate activities in my neighborhood every year, this number seems to hold water. This sort of change will generate a substantial amount of activity in any call center—that's why I chose this example. I am sure every organization will be able to find its own favorite example of frequent customer business transactions.

- Treat me effectively:
  - ➢ Right from the moment I dial in, the CTI/CRM system should know how valuable I am to the bank. So, if it is a busy time for the call center, and I am one of their more profitable and valuable customers, I should get connected and serviced first. This differentiated treatment should be consistent across all channels that I engage in with the bank.

- Be proactive in providing services and sales:
  - ➢ The CSR servicing me should know that I am sharing my credit card with my wife, who also has other accounts with the same bank. However, due to privacy regulations, the CSR cannot tell me what accounts my wife has, and I cannot initiate any address change process on her behalf. Knowing that I have moved, the CSR might want to ask whether my wife would like to be given a reminder to call in and request a change of address. If the answer is positive, the CSR should take the initiative to contact my wife later or have the system send her a reminder to initiate the change of address. In addition, due to the fact that I have moved, the system should provide intelligence to the CSR to sell me additional products. For example, I might need to spend some money to renovate my house or buy furniture. Therefore, I

might be interested in a line-of-credit facility. Alternatively, my credit card limit might be reviewed for an increase, and a different credit card with loyalty points might be offered to me so that I can accumulate some points as well.

If my bank has the necessary infrastructure and operational setup to handle this scenario, it would be a pretty good customer-centric bank. Does your bank pass the "driving test"? Would your business pass the test?

Chapter 2

The Application Agenda Era

Since the early days of computing, organizations have used technology to help automate many of the tedious tasks and business processes that happen every day. Computer applications have been implemented to automate every business process imaginable, from order entry to the billing and fulfillment of customer purchases. Very frequently, these applications are repeated across different products and lines of business (LOBs). Tasks and business processes that used to take months to finish can now be accomplished in minutes. We are doing business in the *application agenda era*.

This same application agenda technological era has resulted in many applica tion silos. A great many silo order entry, billing, and fulfillment systems have been built across various LOBs. When a customer has a problem, such as not getting a product that was ordered, the organization's staff must sign on to multiple systems to find out what went wrong. Some industries, such as banks for example, have managed to incorporate the business automation of manual processes into a single product system—a core banking system for managing direct deposit accounts such as savings and checking accounts. However, as the banking business grows organically or through acquisition, many companies end up with multiple product systems, handling things like credit cards, loans, treasury investments, brokerage accounts, and more. Therefore, managing a customer problem still requires access to multiple sys tems at the same time.

To this day, the application agenda era persists because companies continue to seek technological solutions that will allow them to simultaneously access infor mation from their many silo applications. Front-end applications have been built to automate and exchange information to the silo back-office applications; and to further improve their quest for business automation and improve productivity, more silo applications have been built.

Current IT Infrastructure Situation in Many Organizations

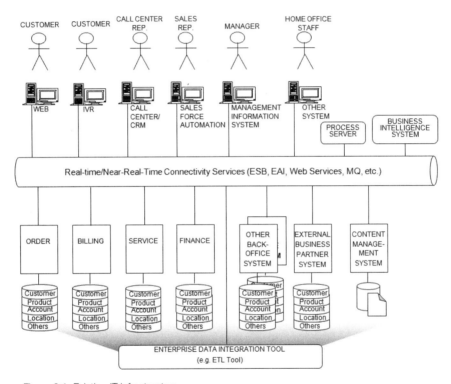

Figure 2.1: Existing IT infrastructure

Figure 2.1 depicts what your existing IT infrastructure might look like. I have segregated the systems into the following categories:

- Back-office systems:

  - These systems help to automate the tasks of managing your products and/or services. These systems capture the description of the products/services, manage supplies, take purchase orders, create accounts, manage deliveries of your products/services, initiate billing cycles, process remittances, and so on. These are your core business processing systems. Some of the more commonly used back-office systems include the Product System, Billing System, Core Business System, Enterprise Resource Planning (ERP) System, Supply Chain Management (SCM) System, Administration System, Accounting System, and Finance System. Traditionally, these are your oldest systems. In some companies, these systems were created back in the 1960s, at the dawn of the computer age, and they have been around since then. ERP and SCM systems are newer. The majority of these were introduced in the late 1980s and 1990s to consolidate the management of resources and supplies. These systems typically run on powerful computers, such as mainframe and mid-range servers. Each of these systems has its own user interfaces for access.

- Front-office systems:

  - These systems are newer, and most were created when the personal computer was entering its maturity stage for business use, during the 1980s and 1990s. The majority of these systems are built to solve problems for front-office workers, typically in sales and customer service. These users must go through many user interfaces to access different back-office systems to do their daily jobs. These front-office systems attempt to offer a platform from which to consolidate access to multiple back-office systems in one place. These are the Customer Relationship Management (CRM) systems for call center automation and Sales Force Automation (SFA) systems that help your distribution channel staffs. Additional features include the component that manages customer information, such as the relationships among customers and customer interactions. Some will also include sales campaign management capabilities or will be integrated with sales campaign systems. Sales campaign systems can also be classified as front-office systems. These typically run on personal computers or mid-range server-based technologies. Each of these systems will have its own user interfaces for access.

- Touch-point systems:
  - With the advent of computer networking and Internet technologies, additional front-office applications encompassing technological devices that allow direct customer contact were implemented. These systems include the Interactive Voice Response (IVR) units that handle phone calls, web-based front-ends to facilitate customer self-servicing via the web, and specialized kiosk machines (e.g., Automatic Teller/Banking Machines—ATM/ABM, for banks). Just as CRM and SFA systems are designed to streamline access for your front-office staff to the back-office systems, these touch-point systems are designed to streamline access for your customers to your internal systems for self-service. A lot of these systems originated in the 1980s and 1990s, when organizations were undergoing cost reductions. In an effort to streamline operations, companies began to look at ways to both automate and to push business processes to their points of origin (i.e., to the end customers and suppliers).

- Integration middleware:
  - Integration middleware was created to connect and allow for communication among all the systems just mentioned, thus enabling them to connect in real-time or in batch.
  - Typical IT jargon used to describe the technology and techniques used in this area include MQ, JMS, Web Services, http, direct-connect, point-to-point, hub-and-spoke, request-response, and many more. Purists in this area will argue that a near-real-time connectivity paradigm exists as well. For simplicity, we will treat near-real-time and real-time connectivity as being the same.

Figure 2.1 depicts an existing IT infrastructure that has business process–focused back-office systems for ordering, billing, service requests, and the like. In some organizations, such as financial services companies, the back-office systems are typically product-focused—e.g., core banking, credit card, brokerage, investment product, life insurance, home insurance, and more. Figure 2.2 depicts the typical IT infrastructure for a financial services company.

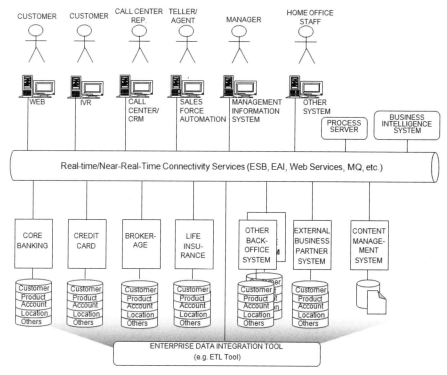

Figure 2.2: Existing IT infrastructure—financial service organization

The Problem

One of the problems with the current IT infrastructure of many organizations is that customer data is spread all over the silo applications (Fig. 2.3).

Using our banking example again, say we have a customer named Robert A.J. Smith. Robert's full name is in the Demand Deposit Account (DDA) system (the core banking system that manages your typical savings and checking accounts), but while applying for a credit card with the bank the name Robert Smith (with out initials) is used. When opening a brokerage account, the name used could be Robert A. Smith (missing the second initial); in a CRM system, the name could be Rob Smith. So, are they the same person? How can your office staff tell?

This is just one simple example using a customer name. In some countries and cultures, customer names may be more precise, but you may have other data problems. For example, Robert may list 1 Main Street as his mailing address in the DDA system, but 2 Main Street as the mailing address in the credit card sys tem. Which one is correct? Maybe 2 Main Street is correct, as Robert has moved next door, but has not yet notified the bank of his change in address. Maybe 1 Main Street is correct, as the person entering Robert's credit card application form made a mistake and typed in 2 instead of 1. Or, maybe both addresses are correct, as Robert lives at both addresses.

When data is held in a silo, data quality problems arise and information cannot be trusted. The same scenario can apply to other information, such as phone num bers, e-mail addresses, and other identifying information associated with Robert Smith. Sometimes, he might use his office phone number. At other times, he might use his home phone number or his mobile phone number.

So, how do we know all these names really belong to the same person? How do we know which address is correct? If we don't, how can we expect to know Rob ert's true household relationships? How can we keep accurate records of his port folio? If we don't know his portfolio, how can we expect to sell more products to him? How do we know how valuable a customer he is? How can we provide dif ferentiated services to our customers if we don't know how valuable they are?

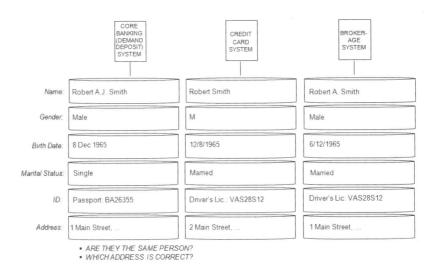

Figure 2.3: Nontrusted customer data across disparate systems

Let's look at a customer service example for the same customer. When Robert A.J. Smith moves and wants to change his mailing address, to how many places must the bank go to change that address? How can it know that it has made all the necessary changes? Typically, the number of products a customer has or uses is one factor reflecting how valuable he is to the business. In this case, the more products this customer has—and the more valuable he is—the more trouble he has to go through just to change his address.

Now, let's look at some up-sell/cross-sell examples using this same banking scenario. When life-changing events, such as moving, marrying, having a baby, or retiring occur, most banks probably already know how to reach you to sell you new products or change existing ones to suit your new circumstances. However, this is not always desirable. Let's assume Robert has just moved. The bank might offer to increase the credit limit of Robert's credit card, thinking that he might need to buy new furniture. Without Robert's data and product portfolio view in one place, the bank may not know that Robert has defaulted on his car loan for many months. In this case, the last thing the bank would want to do is increase his credit limit.

Chapter 3

The Information Agenda Era

Now that many organizations understand that having information in many silo applications will cause data quality issues that impact the way they know and serve their customers, application renewal projects are undertaken every day to build the next generation of back-office applications to automate more processes and products, thus reducing and eliminating some old applications and keeping data in one system. But businesses continue to evolve, with increased merger and acquisition activities, global expansions into other countries, and product diversification. These constantly evolving business activities are changing too fast for IT departments to design and build single systems that can manage everything; the proliferation of applications and data in many silo-based systems is here to stay. To cope with this dilemma, organizations have developed ways to effec tively manage the information in their diverse silo applications.

Managing Information As an Enterprise Strategic Asset

To allow existing back- and front-office applications to automate business pro cesses, organizations are implementing and relying on a new type of technology to manage all the information in these applications. These tools try to unlock the information buried in the silo applications to gain additional insight into manag ing the information as a strategic asset that can be shared.

One technology that organizations have invested in for this approach is Extract Transform Load (ETL) tools, sometimes called enterprise data integration tools.

As the name implies, the major function of this tool is to extract information from a source system, transform the data into the format required by the target system, and then load the data into the target system. While transforming this data, some tools can also standardize, clean, and validate the data to improve its quality. Typically, the data that is so standardized and cleaned includes informa tion such as names (Dave to David), addresses (postal address standard of each country), and phone numbers (correct format of area code, extension, etc.). Some tools will also do record matching to identify unique records. The more sophisti cated tools allow users to store the various data formats and characteristics of these systems, their business definitions, and their transformation rules in a cen tral repository called a *meta-data server*. (Meta-data is a term used in IT to mean the "description of data.") In this way, the details of the information within the system can be referred to and re-used again and again while maintaining consis tency and data quality across all applications.

Other popular technologies include the data warehouse and the data mart. A *warehouse* is a centralized repository of business data that supports analysis and provides additional insights into this data. These warehouses are typically sourced from back- and front-office systems in batch mode at different frequencies (typically daily, weekly, or monthly) depending on business requirements and data availability.

A *data mart* is similar to a data warehouse, but it is designed specifically to help improve the efficiency of a particular type of analysis. For example, you might have a data mart to analyze customer profitability, another to analyze customer propensity to buy another product, and another for customer segmentations. Data from a data mart can come straight from your back- and front-office systems or from your data warehouse (if you have one). Again, like the data warehouse, data mart updates are done in batch mode and at different frequencies, depending on requirements and data availability.

Some organizations have only a data warehouse and run all analyses from there, while others only have specialized data marts to do specific analysis without using a data warehouse. Other organizations employ both data warehouses and data marts.

The introduction of enterprise data integration, data warehouse, and data mart technology has drastically improved the quality and usefulness of the information that was once hidden within silo applications (Fig. 3.1). However, although these technologies are very good at managing and deriving insights from data in bulk, they are used mainly in batch mode, and they may be working on data that is out of date. Today, the expectation is to have access to data in context, in real time. If a problem occurs, such as having two different addresses or two different names, you want to know right away, so that you can resolve the conflict on the spot. Data integration, data warehouse, and data mart technologies do not support this kind of data validation. For example, in the situation cited earlier, with Robert listing an address of 1 Main Street in the DDA system and 2 Main Street in the credit card system, the answer to which one is correct cannot be resolved using these technologies. Even if they can detect the discrepancies, it would be in batch mode, after the fact, and the customer may already be gone. In this case, you would have to manually contact the customer to resolve the potential conflict. Thus, a real-time solution that manages data on an enterprise level is needed to ensure accurate customer data.

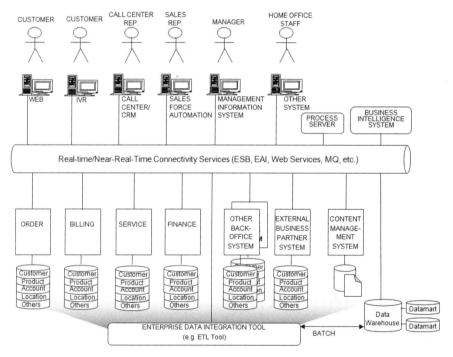

Figure 3.1: Introduction of enterprise data integration tool, data warehouse, and data mart to IT infrastructure

The Birth of MDM for Customer Data

In the late 1990s, businesses sought for a better real-time application to manage customer data at an enterprise level, in order to maintain trusted customer infor mation. Many organizations tried to use client files from back-office applications, Customer Relationship Management (CRM) solutions, or data warehouse solu tions to manage customer data in one place and thus enable their cus tomer-centric initiatives. All these technologies, however, were lacking in one aspect or another.

One of the earliest organizations to use Master Data Management (MDM) was an insurance company, and we'll use this company as an example throughout this chapter. The IT management of this insurance company wanted a better way to manage the customer data shared by their systems. The first thing they did was review all back-office systems and analyze the shared, common customer data, also known as the *master data* (Fig. 3.2). The typical customer data popped up: names, genders, birth dates, addresses, and phone numbers for the people and or ganizations this company was selling to or engaging with. When looking for these common data types, they realized that this data was not only about owners of insurance policies, but also about associated participants such as dependents, beneficiaries, claimants, agents, and others. It became essential to define just who were the "customers" of this business.

It became obvious that, in order to know everything about a customer, all partici pants related to or working with a customer had to be tracked. Therefore, the common data would apply to all participants, instead of to only an individual cus tomer. For simplicity's sake, in this discussion, we will use the word *customer* imply any participant who does any business with an organization. As such, *customer* can mean a prospect, an employee, a business partner, and, in fact, any person or organization who interacts with a particular business.

The insurance company in question decided that if it could get the common party data into one enterprise application and let that application integrate and share data with other applications in the line of business (LOB), data quality would greatly improve. If this new enterprise application could have the intelligence to communicate with other applications, then changes in common data recognized by the Customer MDM could be synchronized across all applications. In this way, there would be a good return on investment (ROI) and once-and-done pro cessing would reduce manual costs. For example, if a customer were to change his address, instead of going to all the systems where this address exists to make the same change, the enterprise Customer MDM would be able to synchronize with other applications, make the change across the boards, and reduce the cost and amount of time spent on this task. In addition, data quality would improve, as the risk of manually entering the wrong data into a system would be eliminated.

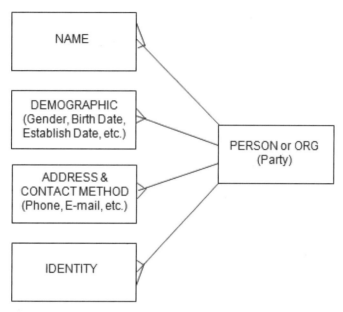

Figure 3.2: Master data: Common participant's data found in all systems.

To do this, a couple more things would have to be added. First, the common data would need a directory structure to identify where else this customer or party data is kept. Thus, a cross-reference with system name and system identifier would have to be included to facilitate communication and synchronization among applications (Figure 3.3).

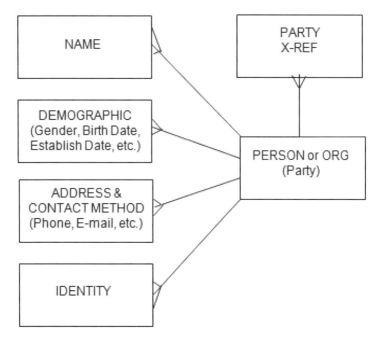

Figure 3.3: Master data: Common participant's data plus cross-reference data.

Second, this solution could not be a simple database. The company would need some services with business rules to surround the common data to ensure that it is clean. These services would also facilitate integration to other applications and have the intelligence to perform two-way synchronization of data when needed.

Having integration and intelligence services in this enterprise Customer MDM solution is not enough to make the information trusted. When you have customer data coming in from so many applications, there must be a way to uniquely iden tify a customer so that there is no repetition in the application. Therefore, ser vices to maintain the integrity of the customer data are required to match and de-duplicate. Based on some matching rules using customer attributes such as name, address, identification number, and the like, this intelligence service can determine whether any incoming customer's records are new or preexisting. If the record is new, then the intelligence service should allow it to be added. If not, previously existing records should be updated. The worst case is when matching is inconclusive. For example, suppose the name and address match, but the iden tification used (e.g., passport number, social security number, etc.) does not. So, is this the same person with different identifications (maybe once using an old passport number and another time using a new one)? Or, are these two different people using the same name, living at the same address? Maybe the two are father and son but the "senior" and "junior" in their names were omitted in the applications. In this case, the system should add the record but mark both as a duplicate suspect with the other and produce a warning message to be resolved at a later date. If they are found to be the same person, the records should be merged together and a decision should be made on which attributes would survive should conflicts occur. At other times, different customer records may merge accidentally, and the system needs a way to split the record into two.

Conflicting customer records require more comprehensive integrity services to manage matching, de-duplication, merge, split, and other operations. These services and requirements only exist when customer data merges from different applications into a new, common application. If the original applications do not have any existing functions or user interface to handle this merging of data, it opens up a new set of business requirements: When you have customer records from different LOBs coming together, which LOB should have jurisdiction to resolve any conflicts? Must a new enterprise department be created to resolve any duplicate records and determine which customer attributes will survive? Data governance (see Chapter 6) must be decided across LOBs, with agreement on who has stewardship over customer records when a conflict arises. As a result, a new data steward user interface that can be used by LOB or enterprise users to manage and resolve duplicate suspects must be created.

The good thing about having all the common customer data in an enterprise Customer MDM solution is that all information is concentrated into a single source. This Customer MDM application can resolve any conflicts and duplications, and uniquely identify a customer record. Return to the case of Robert, who gives 1 Main Street as his address in the DDA system and 2 Main Street in the credit card system. As far as the LOB owning the DDA system is concerned, 1 Main Street is correct, whereas, for the LOB owning the credit card system, 2 Main Street is the correct address. This happens because each LOB does not know that the other has a different address. The conflict will only be detected when the two addresses come together at the enterprise Customer MDM application. Only this application can decide which is correct.

Having common customer data in a single shared application is a good way to improve data quality and get a single version of the truth (i.e., trusted data).

However, this single application still has to serve all LOBs, thus allowing for some unwanted sharing of information: one LOB may access data belonging to another LOB. To prevent this from occurring, access control must be enforced. These rules may be dictated by your company or by government regulations (e.g., privacy acts). Another set of requirements is needed to ensure that this en terprise Customer MDM solution can be deployed and still comply with access control requirements. This application must have an Authorization service to control access by different systems and users to create, read, update, or delete customer data. Different systems and users must be granted rights to use any of the available services and to access any data attributes for each customer record. Together with Integration, Intelligence, and Integrity services, an Authorization service is required to manage and control access to the customers' common and directory data (Fig. 3.4).

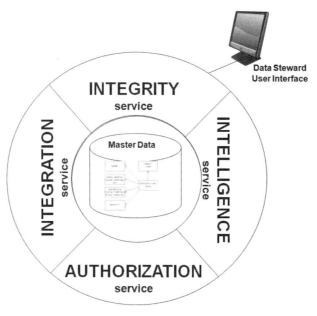

Figure 3.4: Enterprise Customer MDM solution: Master data and services

Based on these functions and features, our example insurance company has a pretty solid enterprise Customer MDM solution for managing a single version of customer data, allowing for a reduced cost by doing once-and-done processing using up-to-date, real-time data in context.

From Business Automation to Business Optimization

Based on the insurance company experience we've just detailed, the Customer MDM solution begins to take shape. From the insurance company example, we now have a definition for master data and master data management. Master data is:

- Common data that is shared and useful to many, if not all, other systems

- Cross-reference or directory data that indicates where the common data came from or where it exists

Master data management is:

- The management of master data to get a single version of the truth

- The usage of master data in context to achieve concrete business benefits through business optimization

The business benefits or ROI for the insurance company was pretty compelling. Operational costs could be reduced by optimizing the business process of customer data by making changes only once. Not bad for a first-phase implementation of any MDM project.

What else could the insurance company, or any other company, do to drive business optimization once it has the basic building blocks of an MDM solution?

Well, insurance companies are all about managing risk and selling protection, and they are always on the lookout for ways to improve their risk management activities. When a new insurance policy application comes in, the underwriter should be able to go to a single place to find the existing insurance coverage ex posure for this new applicant. The last thing an insurance company wants to do is be exposed to over-insurance on any of their customers, defined as a new appli cant already well insured by another insurance policy. Increasing coverage for this person would have the potential to increase the company's claim experience and payout, therefore increasing their risk exposure.

To manage risk exposure, a product portfolio must be added to the Customer MDM solution. A new cross-reference or directory—a product portfolio or ac counts view—must be introduced to increase the value of the Customer MDM solution. Here, we must be very careful as we do not want to replicate all the product information found in various other systems and place that information in the new view. After all, this is not a product system but rather a Customer MDM system. In addition, most data for different products is not common in nature, and thus not suited to the Customer MDM system. When a customer buys a product, a policy or an account is opened. The common data for the different policies or accounts will include its name and type, and the system that is managing it. These are the basic data elements required to get a product portfolio view without duplicating all the data in the MDM system. When required, the product portfolio view can provide the cross-reference or directory data (product/account system name and account number) that shows where detailed product or account infor mation can be found.

To further enhance risk management capabilities, a household view should be used to assess total risk exposures. For example, say Customer A has applied for life insurance coverage naming him as the insured. It would be great if the under writer, through the Customer MDM system, could see that Customer A's spouse also has life insurance and has already taken a big spousal life rider on Customer A. With this information, the underwriter can take the appropriate steps to refuse or reduce the coverage for Customer A if he is over-insured. To support this household view, the relationships among related parties must be managed by this Customer MDM solution. Therefore, Party Relationship data (e.g., parent–child, husband–wife, etc.) must also be introduced as master data (Fig. 3.5).

This insurance company also deals with group life insurance. Companies that sponsor group insurance for their employees can also be tracked. In organiza- tional data, the relationships among the parent and subsidiary companies are an important aspect of managing the total risk exposure for an organization. Unlike personal household relationships, the organizational hierarchies of these group clients are important. The hierarchy construct is slightly different from the rela tionship construct in the sense that there is always an ultimate parent in a hierar chy—you know who is at the top of the hierarchy. Relationship constructs, however, are recursive in nature: there is no hierarchy.

When the risk score of a customer has been determined, it is a good idea to keep track of this new common data in the Customer MDM solution, so that every unit and channel is aware of it. To store the risk scores, the company created a new Party Value area in the Customer MDM solution. Over time, this Party Value area was able to manage many other common and shareable values.

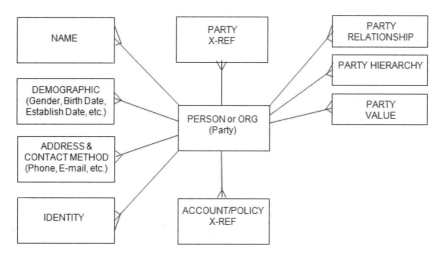

Figure 3.5: Master data: Adding new relationships, hierarchies, values, and account/policy cross-reference data

For insurance and financial services companies, risk management is a very big ROI area. Banks, for example, want to know the total loan offered to a customer before extending another loan, as they would not want to extend a line-of-credit to a customer who has defaulted payment to her credit card with the same bank.

So, from a ROI perspective, using Customer MDM has helped to optimize business in two ways:

- Cost reduction through once-and-done processing

- Improved risk management via trusted, in-context, household views of product exposure information

In improving risk management, the insurance company realized that the same in formation currently in the Customer MDM system (i.e., household and product portfolio information) is also useful in helping to improve up-selling and cross-selling.

The insurance company wanted to know their customers better and improve their communication, services, and sales. They were able to do this using the Cus tomer MDM solution, which can manage information regarding a family or household. In the old days, most companies would have defined *household* people sharing the same house or address, as this was the best data they would have. Even if the company were to know the relationship between two people, there was no system to capture this information. So, if a house has two families (one the owner and the other a tenant), these people are treated as one household, which, from a marketing sense, is not correct. Once the insurance company knows the true family household, the product portfolio of this household can be put in context and this information can assist in more effective up-selling or cross-selling of new products.

With access to full household information as well as the product portfolio of each member of the family, the company now has the basic data to do effective up-selling and cross-selling. Generally, this enriched and trusted information is passed on to data warehouses, data marts, or specialized campaign management applications to determine whether the customer is worth selling to, and if so, what products are most suited to him. For example, if you know your customer is married and has kids, you might want to sell him an education savings plan. However, if you know his spouse has already bought an education savings plan, you might try selling him something else, instead of annoying him by proposing another education plan.

You can run business intelligence and reports on data warehouses and marts to not only determine what to sell, but also to determine the true value of customers. Data values may show customers' profitability, propensity to buy a certain product, propensity to lapse, and other important trends. These values could change the way you service or sell to a customer if they can be made available in real-time to any touch-point system. These values can be loaded into the Customer MDM system as this system becomes operational. Let's assume that the business intelligence reports indicate that Customer A has a "Gold" customer value (very profitable) and Customer B has a "Bronze" customer value (not profitable). If both customers were to call in at the same time, wouldn't it be good if the call center system were able to recognize these customers immediately and give priority to the "Gold" customer?

The insurance company also wanted to improve customer service by tracking its interactions with its customers. This includes all relevant in-bound (e.g., customer calling in) and out-bound (i.e., sales call by agent) communication. The company wanted to ensure that this data did not overlap with the details found in its web or call center systems. Just like the product/account concept, the company only needed to know the high-level, relevant details to better interact with its customers and provide better service. This would prevent embarrassing moments, such as might occur when a customer has just visited the company's website to perform a business transaction and ends up calling the call center shortly after to confirm his status. If the call center agents know that the customer accessed the website earlier, they should be able to go to the appropriate system to find his status. This scenario spurred the creation of an Interaction History subject area within the Customer MDM solution.

In addition, wouldn't it be nice if the various sales campaigns directed at this customer through any channel (such as e-mail, direct postal mail, etc.) were reflected in the Customer MDM system? With this information, the call center agent would be able to remind the customer of any recent sales campaigns that have gone out to him and possibly be able to close the deal while on the line (Fig. 3.6). (One bank has indicated that they can increase their credit card campaign's up take when their call center agents remind customers of a particular campaign mailed to them recently—another solid ROI.)

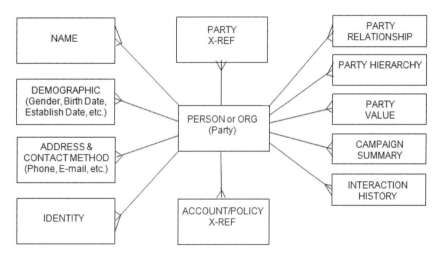

Figure 3.6: Master data: Adding new campaign summaries and interaction history

Let's review our proposed changes to the master data definition perspective and summarize what the ROIs for these changes were. In the example, we introduced the following kinds of data to the Customer MDM:

- Campaign summary data: Similar to product and account data, this should not contain all the campaign details as this is not a campaign management or execution system; only the campaign type, status, timeframe, and channel should be listed

- Interaction history data: A high-level summary of relevant in-bound and out-bound customer interactions

- Customer or party values data: This typically comes from data warehouses or marts that summarize the value of each customer to the organization

This data constitutes a new type of master data that we call *summary* or *consolidated data*. Our master data definition has now expanded to include the following:

- Common data that is shared and useful to many, if not all, other systems

- Cross-reference or directory data that indicates where the common data came from or where it exists

- Summary or consolidated data that is of value

How about our business optimization efforts? What additional benefits or ROIs have we introduced in the example? It is obvious that customer service has improved through the ability to differentiate services by making the summary customer data values available to all touch-points. Knowing all the interaction history also helps. But generally, improvements in customer service are hard to quantify and do not show up in the ROI section. For ROI, the up-selling and cross-selling is optimized by providing account portfolio, summary campaign, and trusted household information to the Customer MDM. Therefore, we have added a third ROI item to our business optimization efforts. The ROIs using Customer MDM now include the following:

- Cost reduction through once-and-done processing

- Improvement of risk management via trusted, in-context, household views of product exposure information

- Improvements in up-selling and cross-selling through trusted family household and product portfolio views, plus integration with business intelligence and campaign systems

Outside Influences on Customer MDM Solutions

Now, let's continue with business optimization, factoring in outside influences that impact the way any company does business. These outside influences in clude laws imposed by government to regulate certain aspects of trade.

One of the main issues facing our hypothetical insurance company is its need to comply with privacy regulations, in terms of the ability to share data across dif ferent LOBs, as well as to obey the solicitation preferences of a customer. Some countries have regulations that forbid one LOB from using customer data from another LOB, while others allow sharing if customer consent has been obtained. Therefore, the rules-of-visibility feature mentioned earlier in the Authorization services to control data access is very important for a Customer MDM solution.

Privacy, as it relates to consent for solicitation, is also tricky to manage. If not done correctly, it can severely impact your sales campaign. Some companies have done it poorly by not differentiating the consent between different products and channels. For example, you can implement a global opt-in/opt-out indicator to track customer solicitation preferences, but often when a customer opts out, she will opt out of every product and channel. That may not be her desire and is certainly not yours. The Customer MDM solution should be designed to allow for differentiated opt-outs based on different product lines and channels. That is, I should be able to call my insurance company to indicate that I do not want to receive any more life insurance campaigns, but that I am open to receiving infomation about other products (i.e., different product lines). I should also have the option of not having campaigns sent to me by mail (I want to be environmen tally friendly), although I am willing to be called—but only at home on Saturday between 2 and 6 p.m. From this range of options, a dedicated subject area to manage privacy and other customer preferences was created within the Customer MDM solution (Figure 3.7).

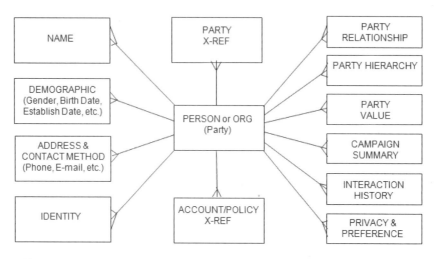

Figure 3.7: Master data: Adding privacy & preferences

Many insurance and financial service companies have adopted Customer MDM to help them comply with government regulations. Enabling Credit Risk reporting is another popular way of using a Customer MDM solution for regulatory compliance, especially for corporate or business banking. Most major banks must comply with a universal credit reporting regulation called Basel II, a complicated credit report that banks must show their local regulators. One of the key differences that separates Basel II from Basel I is the treatment of corporations and their affiliates. It used to be that a bank could report on the total risk exposure of a corporate customer by summing up all the risk exposures of itself and its subsidiaries—the entities within its legal hierarchies (in which they own at least 50% of shares). Under Basel II, the risk exposures now include those from the corporation and other legal entities (including those in which it has less than 50% of shares)—this is called the *operational risk hierarchy* instead of the *legal hierarchy*. As a result, all related legal entities within a corporation must be incorporated into the Customer MDM solution with an operational risk hierarchy to show how they are related. Most banks are able to get the legal hierarchy information easily from an outside data service provider, as this information doesn't change that frequently. However, an operational risk hierarchy is more fluid and difficult to set up. Banks will typically use the legal hierarchy as the starting point and compose the operational risk hierarchy through input from their customer relationship managers. Some entities will naturally fall into multiple operational risk hierarchies. Obviously, this is a very operational function and can change quite frequently. Some banks have tried to use data warehouses or data marts to manage these hierarchies, but the operational nature of this requirement has caused many data management headaches for these companies, because data warehouses and marts are not operational systems, but rather more analytical in design.

Some companies have tried to use the party relationship construct to manage hierarchies. However, the party relationship is infinite in nature and has no obvious parent and child link between two parties, making it very difficult to develop a hierarchy, let alone multiple hierarchies, using this construct. Therefore, a Customer MDM should have a separate construct to manage these hierarchies. If designed well, this could be used for other subject areas as well, instead of just party relationships, and might branch out to include product hierarchies, location hierarchies, and more.

From an ROI perspective, complying with government regulations is typically hard to quantify (unless you get fined) but one of the most compelling events to spur action. Most companies do not want to pay the hefty fines and suffer the negative press exposure that come from not complying with government regulations. The big hammer of the government is always a useful way to justify beginning a Customer MDM project.

So, the ROI effort for business optimization has added a fourth item:

- Cost reduction through once-and-done processing
- Improvement of risk management via trusted, in-context, household views of product exposure information
- Improvements in up-selling and cross-selling through trusted family household and product portfolio views, plus integration with business intelligence and campaign systems
- Assistance in government regulatory compliance, such as pertains to privacy acts and regulatory reporting

Mergers/Acquisitions and the Customer MDM Solution

Before concluding the ROI journey, there is one final ROI that I would like to mention, one that the insurance company encountered. This company has grown through acquisitions and become very good at handling acquisitions, but it still takes them a couple of years on average to combine systems from other organizations. This is typically a very painful exercise and takes a lot of time. If not done properly, it affects customer service and may result in some lost business.

After having implemented the Customer MDM solution, the company realized that the integration effort for new acquisitions was eased as all customer data from the acquired block of business could be put into one system—the Customer MDM system—instead of several. In addition, they were able to leverage this system by first integrating customer data while leaving integration of other data to a later date. This gave their customers the impression that the integration effort was much faster and more seamless and allowed them to enjoy "integrated" ser vice sooner.

Politically, during a merger, an organization that has a running Customer MDM solution is typically at an advantage over an organization that has no Customer MDM solution. It is not too far-fetched in this day and age, assuming systems from both organizations can handle the combined size, to suggest that the surviving systems will be those owned by the organization with the integrated Customer MDM solution.

Now, let's summarize the ROIs from the business optimization effort using Customer MDM:

- Cost reduction through once-and-done processing

- Improvement of risk management via trusted, in-context, household views of product exposure information

- Improvements in up-selling and cross-selling through trusted family household and product portfolio views, plus integration with business intelligence and campaign systems

- Assistance in government regulatory compliance, such as pertains to privacy acts and regulatory reporting

- Expedition of system consolidation during merger and acquisitions, providing a single customer chassis for integration

This concludes the short overview of the creation of a Customer MDM solution through different implementation ideas that optimize business performance and produce measurable ROIs. I hope that this general overview will help you see

how a Customer MDM solution can help your own business become more effi
cient, profitable, and customer-centric. The next few chapters will cover impor
tant topics related to Customer MDM design and implementation.

Chapter 4

MDM for Customer Data

The solution to the problem of achieving a customer-centric business is conceptually simple. One single system must be in place to deal with customer data—the Customer Master Data Management (MDM) system. If data continues to come in from other systems, this Customer MDM system will have the intelligence to know where the data is located and keep it in sync. Therefore, this system will be the place from which all customer data is accessed, and it will be the system of record for this data. It will handle all requests to create, read, update, and delete (typically called CRUD services) data and support multiple ways to search for customer data. Furthermore, it must be linked to all the product sys tems to provide a single product portfolio view, as well as linked to all the touch-point systems (web, call centers, kiosk, etc.) to provide a single interaction view. The system must also ensure that the customer data is clean and without duplicate records, and it must have a data steward user interface to manage dupli cates and to clean data. It should have the intelligence to notify or request other systems to perform tasks based on its customer data (e.g., to notify other systems to synchronize changes; to be proactive in notifying other systems of life-event changes that may result in up-sell or cross-sell opportunities). It must also pro vide the necessary authorization controls, such as rules-of-visibility and entitle ment, to keep data from being accessed and changed by unauthorized users.

Because this will be the most strategic system in your organization, it must be able to scale to meet existing usage and future growth. To do this, it must be able to integrate new attributes or subject areas that may be needed in the future, but it should not use proprietary connectivity protocols to integrate and interoperate with your existing systems.

It is important to remember that master data is not *all* data, but rather only:

- common data that is shared and useful to many, if not all, other systems;
- cross-reference or directory data that indicates where the common data came from or where it exists; and
- summary or consolidated data that is of value.

Master data is protected and managed by a set of services that offers the following capabilities to form a MDM solution:

- Integration (e.g., CRUD services)
- Integrity (e.g., cleansing, matching, and de-duplication)
- Intelligence (e.g., event management and notification)
- Authorization (e.g., rules of visibility and entitlement)

Previous chapters featured a few examples of MDM applications for customer domains. Additional subject areas, such as an Alert feature, may be added to highlight any special messages or notifications that you want everyone to be aware of for a particular customer. These new subject areas must be added with caution, however, and should stay within the confines of the master data definition. If not, your MDM solution will become everything to everyone, and will be too complex to manage and use. If the data is not common and shareable or usable by everyone, then keep it in its home system, where it belongs.
Compare Figure 3.1, which shows an existing IT system infrastructure without Customer MDM, to the new IT systems infrastructure in the Figure 4.1:

With the new Customer MDM system in place, it will be easier to make your business processes customer-centric because you now have an IT infrastructure to support it. Now, whenever customers deal with your business, their data can be placed in the Customer MDM system, which will detect whether these customers are new or existing ones. If they are existing customers, it will not create a new account and it will notify the touch-point system that initiated this request. If they are new customers, a record will be created with a unique key assigned to it. In case of doubt, the Customer MDM system should have a comprehensive process to manage duplicate suspects.

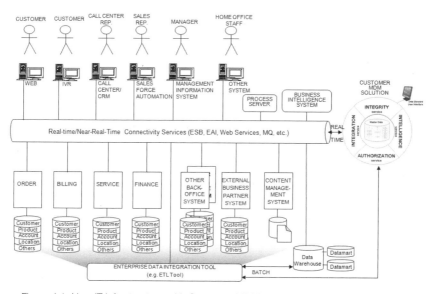

Figure 4.1: New IT infrastructure with Customer MDM solution

With the new Customer MDM system in place, it will be easier to make your business processes customer-centric because you now have an IT infrastructure to support it. Now, whenever customers deal with your business, their data can be placed in the Customer MDM system, which will detect whether these customers are new or existing ones. If they are existing customers, it will not create a new record and it will notify the touch-point system that initiated this request. If they are new customers, a record will be created with a unique key assigned to it. In case of doubt, the Customer MDM system should have a comprehensive process to manage duplicate suspects.

Duplicate Record Management

Duplicate suspects can be managed in many ways. One way is to create a new re cord for the duplicates, marking it as double with an existing record, with the conflict to be resolved at a later date. In this way, there is no delay, because exist ing processes can carry on as if this customer were new. Thereafter, a data stew ard user interface can be created for specialists to see and resolve the duplications. The result could mean that the duplicate suspects are actually the same and therefore should be merged, or that they are not the same and therefore marked as such, so that future duplicate processing will not interfere with these two records again.

Another way is to notify the requesting process that a duplicate has occurred and immediately prompt it for action. This has the advantage of solving the duplication immediately, but this method also has many disadvantages. Processing of subsequent customer records could be delayed while the system is held up resolving the duplication. Existing user interfaces of requesting systems are not likely designed to do this and therefore would need to be changed to handle duplicate suspect processes. The best option for you varies depending on your business process when acquiring new customers or when changing customer information. In some businesses, customer handling is done one at a time through real-time enabled screens.

For example, let's say you go into a bank branch and opening an account. The bank branch officer will sit down with you and go through the creation of you as a new customer in real time. In this case, resolution of duplicate suspects can occur immediately. In other cases, new customer data records might come in batches. For example, when you apply for a credit card, you fill out a form and send it to the bank. Your application, together with thousand of others, is processed in a back-room operation without real-time direct interaction with you. The customer records are approved as a batch and then set up in a batch file and loaded to the bank credit card processor.

To be efficient, a bank needs both methods of resolution: one to handle in-person, one-on-one customer interactions, and one to handle batch-processed interactions.

Because the Customer MDM system will introduce new processes to your organization, such as a duplicate suspect process and a whole data governance process (who is responsible for resolving customer data conflict, how it should be resolved, etc.; see Chapter 6), to fully leverage a Customer MDM system to enable customer-centric processes, your existing customer handling processes will most likely have to change. As a result, changes to existing touch-point and back-office systems will probably have to be made.

One thing's sure: If you are going to undertake a complete overhaul of your IT infrastructure and business processes in one big-bang project, the odds of success are against you. As with any change, try to do it in incremental steps, with each step providing value in terms of positive return on investment (ROI). In Chapter 3, you saw how the Customer MDM solution was implemented in phases by an insurance company. Chapter 5 will present some additional ideas on where and how to go about phasing in a Customer MDM solution for your organization.

What Else You Need

Here, we'll explore in more detail other issues that you must resolve in your quest to establish a Customer MDM system and a customer-centric organization.

Data Load - ETL

Once you have a Customer MDM solution in place, the master data already in various back- and front-office systems must be moved (or at least copied) into the Customer MDM system in order be useful. This typically involves an initial massive bulk load of data in batch mode. Subsequently, if master data still occurs in any of the front- and back-office systems that cannot be reflected in the MDM solution in real time, the new master data or changes to existing data will also need to be loaded on a periodic basis; this process is called the *delta load*

In the old days, bulk data movements like the initial and delta loads were done using customized programs especially developed for each source system. This involved painstaking work to figure out the format of the data in the source system so that it could be extracted. After that, data transformation had to occur to make sure that the data was in a format understood by the MDM solution—the target. Finally, the data was loaded into the MDM solution using the same programs or through other tools. Although slow and complicated, this old way still works, and many companies still use it.

Thankfully, however, many software companies now offer applications that can simplify the extract, transform, load (ETL) processes to simplify and speed up bulk data movement processes in batch.

Data Quality – Data Standardization and Cleansing

Two of the main data elements in an MDM solution, and especially in Customer MDM, are name and address. Name and address are also key data elements in identifying a person or company. They are used for everything from searching for a customer, to comparing whether one customer is similar to another. Names and addresses seem like simple things, but, with all the differences of cultures and places that the average business deals with, variations of the same name and address can crop up. For example, names such as David can be shortened to Dave, John can be Jack, Margaret can be Maggie or Peggy, and IBM Corp. can be International Business Machine Corporation or IBM Inc. Addresses such as Unit 12, 1 Main Street, Toronto, ON can be 1 Main St., Unit #12, Toronto, Ontario. These variations will cause problems if we use them for searching, identifying, and matching parties.

Standardization "levels the playing field" by making all variations correspond to a single set format. So, next time we're given a name like Peggy, we might want to standardize it to both Maggie and Margaret, so that these names will match up in the MDM solution. Similarly, if given 1 Main St., we want it to match up with 1 Main Street. A standardization tool will produce tremendous payback on improving search time and matching accuracy.

Supplementary Data Sources

Once we begin to load customer data into one single MDM solution, we aren't limited simply to data we gather from systems within our organization. Many businesses buy additional customer data to supplement what they don't have, in order to improve data quality. Many companies specialize in providing additional data about different parties. A few well-known ones include ACXIOM, Experian, and D&B (a.k.a., Dun & Bradstreet). These companies can help you to clean up your existing data (e.g., standardize addresses for you), and they can provide supplementary data that might be useful for your organization. Some examples of supplementary data include previous addresses, relationships (family and employer/employee), line of business, and other details.

Integration Middleware

As mentioned earlier, one of the key ways to harvest the power of a MDM solution to transform the way your organization does business in a customer- and product-centric way is to integrate the solution to the rest of the systems in real-time mode. The good news is that there are many ways to integrate systems together in real-time. When only a handful of systems are involved, point-to-point integration among the systems will work. But, when you are dealing with a large number of systems – more than four, it is worth investigating and using more elaborate integration middleware to connect all these systems together. Integration middleware and integration formats include Enterprise Service Bus (ESB), Enterprise Application Integration (EAI), and more. The one you choose depends on the number of systems you need to connect and the connectivity style you select.

For example, let's take a situation in which an address for a party is changed in the MDM solution, and the address change has to be replicated to multiple systems that still need to keep track of that address. When the party address change is made in the MDM solution, the MDM solution can send the change to the integration middleware, which in turn can broadcast this change to all appropriate systems (known as the *push-and-forward* method). Alternatively, the integration middleware can take the change and place it in a queue—instead of broadcasting the change to all systems, individual systems can subscribe to changes on individual queues and only go to the queue to pick up the change when notified of that a change has occurred (known as the *publish-and-subscribe* method). The method you select will depend on your company's needs and your existing system environment.

Where and How To Start

Assuming that you have made the decision to proceed with implementing a MDM solution to help your organization achieve a customer- and product-centric operation, the next question will be where and how to start. The days of mega-projects that are mega expensive and mega long are over. Not many organizations have the appetite to spend millions of dollars and wait many years to see the result of implementing a new system. These types of projects are seldom successful due to many factors including and not limited to:

- Change in key project sponsors and staff resulting in the derailment or cancellation of the project

- Change in business requirements and priorities

- Inability to keep a team focused on a long project

- Project management complexities that occur with too many resources and overly long timelines

Performing a phased implementation has many benefits. This will be a complex project and invariably mistakes will be made along the way. So, if we keep each phase of the project small and short, we can contain mistakes more effectively and correct them before we embark on subsequent phases.

Spending some time deciding on how to phase in your MDM solution will reap valuable rewards; most long and involved "big-bang" approaches result in a "big bust." Typically, to maximize success, plan for a first-phase implementation that takes no more than six months and can deliver some tangible values to the orga nization at that time. Subsequent phases can vary from five to nine months, de pending on the problems being solved and what values will be achieved.

Many factors should be considered when it comes to determining the scope of the first phase. Some of the key factors are:

- Which line of business (LOB) should we start with?
  - Try to start with only one, if possible.

- Which back-office system(s) should we integrate with?
  - Try to start with only one, if possible.

- What channel systems should we integrate with?
  - Pick a channel with minimal exposure to external clients, so that you have more control. For example, pick call center over web channel enablement; you'll be learning by doing, and you don't want clients exposed to any mistakes or problems. Because the call center systems are operated by internal staff, they can provide a layer of insulation to hide rough patches until you get them smoothed out.

- Should it be real-time, batch integration, or both?
  - Try batch integration if you can find enough value with this approach to support your first phase. This minimizes system complexity and gives your organization a chance to review and resolve data quality issues. If not enough value can be realized in batch mode, consider implementing real-time access for one channel, say the call center, and with limited views instead of fully transactional.

- What architecture styles should you start with?
  - There are multiple architecture styles; these are explored further in the next section.

Implementation Style and Approach

John Radcliffe, Andrew White, and David Newman of Gartner have defined four architecture styles for MDM (Fig. 4.2): consolidation, registry, co-existence, and transactional. The definitions for these styles will give you a perspective on how to approach your MDM solution implementation.

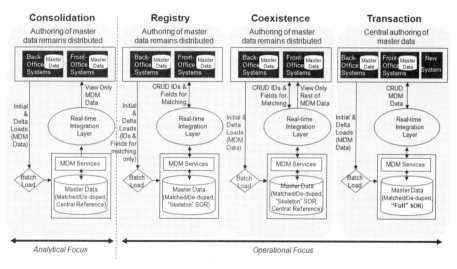

Figure 4.2: Interpretation of Gartner's four architecture implementation styles

The *consolidation style* mainly involves the aggregation of master data after the fact, mainly in batch, with data not guaranteed to be up-to-date. This new physical store of master data is generally used to support analysis and is not operationally focused, as the other three styles are. This approach resembles an operational data store in a data warehouse, but with limited data domains and with real-time access. Authoring of master data remains distributed among the source systems.

During implementation, master data from source back- and front-office systems is loaded in batch to the MDM system. During the batch load, the master data is standardized and matched to determine duplicate suspects. This process can be accomplished using an ETL tool or by the MDM system. The limited master data in the MDM system is then made available for view only through a few user interfaces. This is a good way to find out how good, bad, or ugly your master data looks after it is consolidated in one place. If desired, the duplicate suspects can be reviewed and merged if they are found to be real duplicates (or remain separated if they are different entities). This is typically conducted using a data steward user interface provided by the MDM system. The authority to conduct data steward functions is typically limited to a selected group of user. All other users are restricted to viewing the data only. Any additions or changes to existing master data are conducted in batch mode via periodic batch delta loads.

The *registry style* manages, in the MDM solution, the identifiers of the customer data records found in the various disparate systems, The MDM solution will generate a unique ID that will be the lynchpin ID to provide cross-references to all other identifiers. A consolidated view is typically achieved by consolidating all the records from their source, using the identifiers in a virtual way. This is the most lightweight of the three operationally focused styles of MDM architecture and is the easiest to implement. Authoring of the master data is still distributed and done outside the MDM system.

During implementation, not all master data from source back- and front-office systems is loaded. Only the various IDs and any fields that can assist in matching and duplicate suspect detection are loaded in batch to the MDM system. For individual entities, the matching fields typically consist of name, address, birth date, gender, and some form of identification (e.g., social security number, national registration number, or passport number). For organizational entities, the matching fields typically consist of name, address, and some of identifier (e.g., taxation number or company registration number). During the batch load, the limited master data is standardized and matched to determine duplicate suspects. This process can be accomplished using an ETL tool or by the MDM system. The master data in the MDM system is then made available for not only viewing, but also adding and updating through some user interfaces or real-time access by different systems. If desired, the duplicate suspects can be reviewed and merged if they are found to be real duplicates (or remain separated if they are different entities) using a data steward user interface provided by the MDM system. Any additions or changes to existing master data can still be conducted in batch mode via periodic delta loads.

In registry style, the authoring of master data is still done outside the MDM system and therefore can still create data quality issues. For example, if Kelvin Looi's home address is 1 Main Street in source system A and 2 Main Street in source system B, which one is correct? Is system A correct due to a typing error when entering the address in system B? Is system B correct, as Kelvin has moved to 2 Main Street and his address in system A has not been corrected? Maybe both

are correct, as Kelvin owns both 1 Main Street and 2 Main Street, and both sys
tem A and B can only store one address each. MDM solutions that use the regis
try approach may be able to provide some indication of the level of confidence
for the correct address in each system, but this generally cannot resolve the sce
nario when both addresses are correct.

The *co-existence style* keeps track of not only the identifiers but also a copy of
the customer records in the centralized physical store of the master data. Au
thoring of this data is still distributed and conducted at the source systems. But a
consolidated view is now achieved without having to retrieve the data from the
multiple source systems when needed. It is in one place. This saves the subscrib
ing system the time and effort needed to retrieve and consolidate data from multi
ple systems on the fly. But, since authoring is still conducted at source systems,
there will still be the same quality issues as in the registry style. The co-existence
style is generally of greater value to organizations than is the registry style, but it
is more difficult and takes longer to implement.

During implementation, all master data from source back- and front-office systems is loaded. During the batch load, the master data is standardized and
matched to determine duplicate suspects. Again, this process can be accomplished using an ETL tool or by the MDM system. The majority of master data in
the MDM system is for viewing only, except for that data mentioned in registry
style. Just like the registry style, the IDs and matching fields are made available
for not only viewing, but also adding and updating through some user interfaces
or real-time access by different systems. Again, if desired, the duplicate suspects
can be reviewed and merged if they are found to be real duplicates (or remain
separated if they are different entities) using a data steward user interface pro
vided by the MDM system. Any additions or changes to existing master data can
still be conducted in batch mode via periodic delta loads.

The authoring of most of the master data is still distributed, so the co-existence
style implementation can still create the same data quality issues identified in the
registry style. The only advantage the co-existence style has over the registry
style is that the master data can be viewed entirely within the MDM system, in
stead of having to be pulled on the fly from various systems.

The *transactional style* is the most comprehensive architecture style, as it not
only keeps track of all the data in the centralized physical store but also controls
the authoring capabilities of the master data in this central location. All the

source systems can still keep a copy of the master data if they want to; this data will integrate with the MDM solution, in real-time or batch, which will have ad ditional capabilities to author the data to keep it clean and unique and to allow multiple entries of the same data types when permitted. For example, System A and System B might still have their own rules to keep Kelvin Looi's address as 1 Main Street and 2 Main Street, respectively. But, when the two addresses are sent to the MDM system, that system will have authoring rules to determine whether 1 Main Street is correct, 2 Main Street is correct, or both are correct. This might require automated workflow and/or manual intervention to make the determina tion, but the final results are kept in the centralized MDM solution. So, the MDM solution holds the "golden" copy of Kelvin's true address, not System A or Sys tem B. Both of these systems are merely the source of the address(es).

A good transaction-style MDM solution should also have capabilities to store and manage new enterprise-level data that is currently not found in any other systems. For example, customer privacy preferences across the enterprise may not be stored anywhere else; this provides an example of a good new data domain to be stored and managed by the MDM solution. Some companies may have designated a call center system to be the master system to store privacy preferences, but this ap proach is problematic when you have more than one call center system or you want to make the privacy preferences shared across multiple channels. A call center sys tem may not be able to share the data readily with other channel systems, such as web and sales force automation, and with other back-office applications.

During a transaction-style implementation, all master data from source back- and front-office systems is loaded. Similar to the co-existence style, during the batch load, the master data is standardized and matched to determine duplicate suspects using an ETL tool or by the MDM system. All the MDM data is made available for not only viewing, but also for adding and updating through some user inter faces or real-time access by different systems. Again, if desired, the duplicate suspects can be reviewed and merged if they are found to be real duplicates (or remain separated if they are different entities) using a data steward user interface provided by the MDM system. Once the MDM data is loaded, typically any changes are conducted in real-time via user interfaces or access to different sys tems. Periodic batch delta loads are still supported for those systems that do not support real-time access.

In the case of transactional style, the data quality of the MDM data is optimal and is treated as the new system-of-record. Another huge advantage to this style is that, in the future, if you are developing another application that requires master data, you don't have to design and keep another copy of the master data in the new application. You can simply manage the master data via real-time access to the MDM system. It's important to keep as few copies of master data as you can in the future. The more copies you have, the more problems you will have in keeping the data in sync, and this impacts data quality.

Phase 1 Implementation Consideration

Now that you have some ideas of the four different implementation styles (Fig. 4.2), you can mix and match the styles for your phased implementations. You can go through different styles one phase at a time. For example, you can start with the registry style to master the cross-reference data in Phase 1. After that, in Phase 2, you can add more data to the Customer MDM hub using a co-existence style, where the authoring of the data still occurs at the source systems. Finally, in later phases, you can start to change your business process by changing to transactional style, in which all data in the Customer MDM hub becomes the master data, and the Customer MDM hub is responsible for authoring.

Another approach might be to start with a consolidation style to get all the needed data in one spot—the Customer MDM hub—and let all users in the organization have access to it to see how good, bad, or ugly the data is. After getting users familiar with seeing customer data from a central source, you can now start Phase 2, in which customer data owners agree to reposition their business process so that the authoring process starts in the Customer MDM hub and data contained in the hub is recognized as trusted—as in the transactional style.

You can even mix different implementation styles within a single phase. For ex ample, you can start with the registry style, since it is simpler to implement for Phase 1. But, this approach might not provide you with enough business value to satisfy your business users and management. So, while performing the mastering of cross-reference data, you might want to add in the mastering of new transactional data, such as customers' privacy preferences. The privacy prefer ence data in this Phase 1 Customer MDM solution will then become the only authoring source for all LOBs for this customer. Therefore, you are mixing regis try style (to manage the cross-references) and transactional style (to manage the privacy preference) in Phase 1 to help drive additional business benefits.

Sometimes, it might be desirable to just go with a full transaction-style approach in Phase 1 for all customer data. Typically, this approach is used during systems replacement. For example, a company might use the Customer MDM solution to replace the old Client Information File (CIF) system that outlived its usefulness. Or, using the banking example, let's assume a bank wants to replace the existing core banking system with a new one. While implementing the new system, the bank takes the opportunity to add in a Customer MDM solution to supplement its new core banking solution, so both can be implemented at the same. They will then, through this core banking replacement project, have a robust and flexible Customer MDM solution that can also manage other LOB data in real-time.

Other than considering different implementation styles, you also need to consider how data is going to get into the Customer MDM solution. Typically, most com panies, approximately 80% from my experience, will use the traditional ETL batch process to load in the bulk of their customer data from different source sys tems to the Customer MDM solution during Phase1.

Some more innovative companies might use a continuous conversion method for their Phase 1 load to the Customer MDM system (Fig. 4.3). These companies will initially install the Customer MDM solution with no customer data in it. When it goes live, and as new customer data comes in, in real-time, one record at a time, it will be persisted and managed in the Customer MDM solution. This ap proach might make sense for your business. It is simpler to execute, as you don't have to worry about massive bulk loads of data from multiple sources in Phase 1, and you don't need to handle and resolve the potentially duplicated customer data that might arise from these massive loads. As one IT executive in one organiza tion told me, "I don't want to be responsible for dealing with the potential tens or hundreds of thousands of duplicate customer data that might arise after I load all my customer data into the Customer MDM hub in one weekend. I really don't know how to deal with it, and my business users will not be geared up to manage and resolve so many duplicates. I would rather have them resolve each one as it arises—when new customer comes in, or when an existing customer contacts us. I would then store or move their data into the Customer MDM hub and let the person managing that data at that time resolve any data conflicts right on the spot."

The continuous conversion approach might makes sense to you for Phase 1, but of course you will not have the benefit of all customer data in a single place at once. Of course, in later phases, when your business organization is geared up for the massive load, you can load the remaining customer data using the ETL load approach.

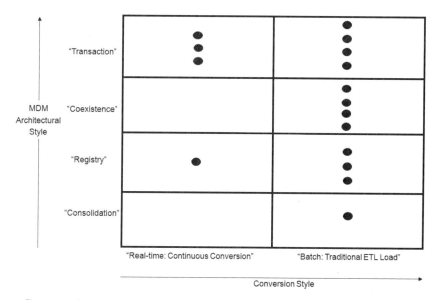

Figure 4.3: Sampling of 16 companies' Phase 1 approach to implementation styles and data conversion methods

Regardless of how you choose to implement your Customer MDM solution, the final results will be a more customer-centric business that is keenly and insightfully in touch with its customers and clients. The benefits of the Customer MDM solution far outweigh any costs or difficulties in its implementation: in creased productivity, better response time, and an individualized approach to cus tomer service.

Chapter 5

How Other Organizations Use MDM for Customer Data: Case Studies

Let's now review some case studies in which the Customer Master Data Management (MDM) concepts described so far have been applied. We will start with a few banking cases, followed by cases from other sectors such as manufacturing, telecommunications, and insurance.

Banking

Let's first look at three banking scenarios: Retail Bank CIF, Commercial Bank Customer MDM Implementation, and an ATM Channel Implementation.

Retail Bank CIF

This is the case of a multi-line bank. This bank grew by many acquisitions over the past twenty years. It currently has more than 100 million accounts throughout its retail business segment, including checking and savings accounts, credit card accounts, loan accounts, and more. Over the years, as it acquired many other companies, it ended up with more than 20 different client files. Some of the companies acquired have up to three client files; for example, one for savings and deposit business, one for credit card business, and one for brokerage business.

The bank's strategy many years ago was to consolidate all data into one client file. As one business executive said, "I don't want 23 versions of my customer. I want one version." The bank's IT department decided to pick one client file from among all available to be the sole surviving "master file." However, the IT department couldn't find any one client file that was robust enough and acceptable to all lines of business (LOBs), for both practical and political reasons (everyone wanted their client files to be the chosen one). In the end, the bank finally compromised and decided to use the client component of the call center Customer Relationship Management (CRM) solution as the client file.

The company undertook a client-file consolidation project that lasted many years. It stopped after the company had consolidated and discarded many of the smaller client files, leaving five of the biggest. The project was halted because the bank had just acquired another bank of about half its size, and the volume of customer data had increased tremendously since the project started. The call center client component chosen wasn't robust enough to scale to that volume. Also, throughout the consolidation period, the number of new channels (web, ATM, branch platform system, etc.) requesting access to the customer data in real-time also increased. The call center client component was able to handle the call center real-time integration and the traditional batch integration of data from the rest of the channels, but it was in no way designed to integrate with all the channels in real-time.

The bank still believed in the benefits of having one single client file—it just didn't have the right solution. Management decided to try a Customer MDM solution to replace the call center client component. This was a system replacement approach, and all the data was migrated in batch mode to the new Customer MDM solution from the call center client components and the remaining client files. Now, customer data in the Customer MDM hub is the master data from a transactional-style perspective for all retail banking business.

Commercial Bank Customer MDM implementation

Our next case study is a commercial bank. This commercial bank has approximately 1 million customers across different LOBs, such as corporate finance, cash trade, real estate loans, equipment leasing, and so on. This Customer MDM solution was driven by the need to comply with government regulations rather than by a need for better direct customer interactions: The bank had to comply with the new Basel II risk-compliance regulation within a certain timeframe. The company had about 23 different product systems to manage its commercial customers.

Management's original idea, like that of so many other banks, was to load all customer data from the 23 customer data sources and the risk scores (loss given default, propensity for defaults, etc.) needed for Basel II reporting to the data warehouse. Then the data warehouse, using the necessary reporting tools, would produce the needed reports. But one of the key requirements to Basel II is the ability to report customer risk based on an operational risk hierarchy. This hierarchy must be constructed, as it is not present in any of the source systems. If the bank used the data warehouse as storage, it would now have to operationalize data warehouse usage. Therefore, it would have to construct the business logic on the data warehouse and create new operational screens to manage de-duplication of customer data; access control to make sure only authorized users can view, add, and change data; new user interfaces to allow creation of the operational hierarchies, and the like.

The data warehouse was never meant to do all this; managing operational risk hierarchies is a very operational function, because these hierarchies changes all the time—every day client companies diversify, buying or selling other companies. A data warehouse is not really meant to perform operational functions. The company considered operationalizing some of the analytical values created by the warehouse so they would be accessible to the business in real time, but building a whole new business logic infrastructure around the data warehouse was not something the bank wanted to do.

It was decided to use a Customer MDM solution instead, making it the system of record for this operational risk hierarchy data. The Customer MDM solution was designed as the hub for managing operational risk hierarchies. The bank loaded all customer data from its 23 product systems into the Customer MDM solution. It then created a user interface for a group of users within the compliance office. These users are allowed to enter and change customers' operational risk hierarchies. All other users, such as the client relationship managers (CRMs) managing customer accounts, can view the data to make sure it is correct. The CRMs can create their own marketing or sales hierarchies for their customers, but any changes to the operational hierarchies, such as adding a new customer, new ownership structures, or the like, must be directed to the compliance office user group. These changes affect the operational risk hierarchy data that will be used for Basel II compliance reporting, and it's essential that only qualified users have access to this information.

The operational risk hierarchies with associated customer details is now the source of all customer data to be loaded to the data warehouse. The data ware house still receives the products, accounts, and associated risk scores from the 23 product systems, and it can generate mandatory Basel II compliance reports using data from all the product systems and trusted customer data with associated oper ational risk hierarchy data from the Customer MDM solution.

This Customer MDM solution is now the customer master. In later phases, the same Customer MDM solution helped streamline the whole on-boarding of new commercial customers and credit risk checking for this commercial bank, acting as the single trusted source of customer data, and thus fulfilling the ideal of a regulatory compliance–driven first-phase project.

ATM Channel Implementation

Another multi-line bank has done a pretty decent job of consolidating its customer data into CIF system client files over the past twenty years. The CIF is using older technology and is hard to change, but it still provides a decent view of the retail customer data, although a lot of the data is loaded in batch mode every night.

About ten years ago, the bank created another CIF for its corporate banking busi ness, to manage organizational data and the associated key stakeholders (CEO, CFO, etc.) of these organizations. This CIF was created using newer technology and was easier to change, but it was designed to be corporate customer–centric.

Although customer data is pretty well managed and generated using only two CIFs, the bank started encountering business challenges that it needed to resolve, and the two CIFs could not provide solutions. One challenge was that the bank didn't have a complete view of all its customers, especially the key stakeholders of its corporate customers, which happen to be one set of its best customers. For example, John Doe may be the CEO of a big corporate customer of this bank. But, if he did not put a lot of cash into his savings account at this same bank, he may not receive VIP treatment when he visits the retail banking business, since the two CIFs are not sharing data with each other.

Also, it is very apparent that, over the last ten years, the company's customer base is using more channels to conduct business with the bank. In the old days, the customer typically walked into the bank to do business; nowadays, the bank ing interaction could be via ATM, web, or call center. The old CIFs were de signed to integrate with a core banking system, with usage from the branch channels. Now, other channels want equal real-time access to the customer data, in order to maintain the customer relationship and service quality level.

The CIO realized that the two CIFs had to be combined into one, and that this sole CIF needed to be flexible enough in its architecture to support all real-time access demands to the customer data. After evaluating the pros and cons of se lecting one of the existing CIFs to be the ultimate CIF, the CIO decided that nei ther could do the work required to handle the new flexibility. He decided instead to implement a new MDM solution, which would then act as the ultimate CIF.

As details of the implementation were discussed, however, it became very appar ent that it would be impossible to undertake a "big-bang" approach to replace ei ther of the old CIFs. Each CIF had more than 100 other programs and interfaces interacting with it on any single day. Redirecting all this traffic to the new Cus tomer MDM solution would be a gigantic task, possibly taking years. In re sponse, the CIO came up with a "surround-and-sunset" approach to replace the two CIFs. Whenever a new IT project required access or changes to the CIF, the new Customer MDM solution would be used instead. Over time, access to the old CIFs would be redirected to the new Customer MDM solution, one project at a time. Once all interfaces were redirected, the old CIFs would be retired.

It happened that the next project to come along after this "surround-and-sunset" strategy was proposed was an ATM replacement scheme. The bank wanted to roll out a new series of graphical user interface–based ATMs to replace its old character-based ATMs.

When using the old ATM, a customer performing a weekly cash withdrawal of the same amount typically needed to go through the following steps;

- Push the ATM card into the slot

- Choose the available language preference, if different from that displayed

- Enter the personal identity number (PIN) or pass code to display a series of menu options

- Select the menu option (e.g., cash withdrawal)

- Select the amount (e.g., $100)

- Select the account to withdraw from (e.g., savings account)

- Select option on "Do you want to print receipt?"

This is six or seven steps (depending on whether you selected a different language preference) to withdraw the same amount every week, yet this represents a very typical ATM transaction.

The bank wanted to use the Customer MDM solution to store the customer details required by the ATM. So, when the typical customer does the same weekly transaction again using the new ATM system for the first time, the first thing the new ATM machine does is go to the old system, get the customer's data, and transfer it to the Customer MDM solution (a continuous conversion approach). It then guides the customer through the same tasks as before to withdraw money. The difference is that, at the end of the cash withdrawal transaction, the ATM asks whether the customer wants to save these option choices as a "favorite transaction." If the customer chooses "yes," this new preference information will be kept in the Customer MDM hub, together with other information it received, such as language preference, available account types and IDs, and more.

The next time this customer uses the new ATM, his data, including his preference data, will now be retrieved from the Customer MDM solution. The new weekly cash withdrawal now looks something like this:

- Push the ATM card into the slot. The right language will be displayed, based on the customer's last transaction (language preference details from the Customer MDM solution)

- Enter the PIN or pass code, to display a series of menu options, with "Favorite Transaction – Cash Withdrawal $100" as the top option

- Select "Favorite Transaction – Cash Withdrawal $100". The customer gets his money immediately, without being asked about a printed receipt because the Customer MDM solution remembers his preferences

The customer's weekly cash withdrawal is cut down to three steps—a 50% efficiency improvement.

This very simple idea shows positive return on investment (ROI) through re duced transactions and increased customer satisfaction (quicker turnaround and lower queue time). At the same time, the system converts data one record at a time to the Customer MDM solution, without a massive data load. The customer data kept in this Customer MDM hub can also be used by other channels in fu ture projects. For, example, the customer language preference can be used by the web channel so that the correct language pages are loaded automatically when a customer signs on, and calls by this customer to the call center can be routed to a person with matching language skills.

Telecommunications

Our next case study involves a telecommunications company with four LOBs—land line, Internet, television, and mobile phone. Its customer data is stored in many disparate systems, including three separate billing systems (one for land line and Internet, a separate one for television, and the last one for mo bile phone). Over the years, this company has implemented many IT projects to streamline its operation and improve its business process. For example, it has consolidated multiple product-based call centers into two, one for retail and one for enterprise customers. It has also created a one-bill-only system so that cus tomers can combine many accounts together into one single bill and get a dis count, a method used by many telecommunications companies to bundle accounts and tie customers in so they won't drop any one account. It also has an enterprise data warehouse, where it stores the entire bulk of customer and ac count data. The reliability of the customer data is suspect, however, because, un like banking and insurance, telecommunications companies do not have a lot of data about a customer—these businesses only need name, address, a piece of ID, and a credit card to open an account. So, matching and merging customer records into a data warehouse may not result in accurate information.

Due to the intense competition with other telecommunications companies, this company needed to look at ways to understand its customers better, including their total household relationships and the associated accounts they, as a com bined household, have with this company. Using improved customer data, this telecommunications company wants to enable their call center representatives to have a complete view of the customers they are dealing, with including all their household and account information. In this way, they can increase customer sat isfaction during service time and be able to use the information to drive more precise, relevant, and effective sales campaigns to up-sell or cross-sell the right products. They want to be able to provide more competitive bundling based on household information, rather than based on the individual and her accounts.

This telecommunications company decided that a centralized customer master file using a Customer MDM solution was the key to getting a more complete view of customer values and achieving a more customer-centric business. For its Phase 1 project, it consolidated the customer data from all billing systems (viewed as the most accurate and complete) for all products into the Customer MDM solution. This Customer MDM solution will cleanse, merge, and de-duplicate as much as it can based on the limited customer data (typically name, address, ID, and cross-reference to where the data exists in the LOB bill ing systems—a typical registry-style approach) it gets from the billing systems. Because the customer data is limited, this company decided not to undertake any automatic collapse of customer data, even in the instance of duplicates, because it has no confidence in the data quality and it also wants consent from its customers before merging their records. (Some customers may decide, for privacy reason, that they don't want one LOB to use data from another LOB.)

The Customer MDM solution was also connected to the call center solution. So, when a customer calls in, the call center solution calls the Customer MDM solution. If the Customer MDM solution identifies that this customer is potentially a duplicate with another, the call center rep is trained to ask the right probing questions to ascertain whether these two records are the same. If they are, the rep can ask the customer for permission to combine the records to allow sharing of data across LOBs. Over time, duplicates will be resolved and customer data quality will improve. This is Phase 1.

In Phase 2, the capabilities of the Customer MDM solution were increased to al low capture of customer privacy preferences, marketing solicitation preferences, and household relationships if known. For example, during a call, the call center rep might learn that another person having the same address is really a spouse (or parent or child), and she can then capture the relationship data appropriately.

In Phase 3, the customer data in the Customer MDM solution becomes the main trusted source of customer data to feed the data warehouse. The data warehouse, with its associated campaign data marts, can then churn out the right marketing campaign for existing customers. The campaign data is transferred to the sale campaign system for execution, and some of the data also goes to the Customer MDM solution to identify that an active sales campaign is under way for this customer. So, if the customer happens to contact the call center about this sales campaign or for any other matter, the call center rep will know in advance that the sales campaign is on and she will be able to execute the right process to in crease the success rate of this campaign.

Insurance

In this case study, a multi-line insurance company wants to transform into an in tegrated financial services company, offering not only traditional life insurance and property & casualty insurance products, but also all sorts of investment vehi cles, including banking and brokerage products. Its CEO wants to differentiate this company from other, more product-centric companies. This CEO wants his insurance company to be known for its customer-centric process, and a key to this strategy is to consolidate operations on customer data in one place, using a Customer MDM solution.

Like other companies, the insurance company knows that it cannot accomplish this project in one big bang. It has to be done in phases, and each phase must pro duce positive ROI before it can proceed.

The first phase targeted the life insurance division. This division alone has cus tomer data stored in more than 30 different systems. Getting all the data in from all these systems was a massive task in itself. This company's unique approach was to stipulate that if customer data is in the Customer MDM solution, it should not be in any other systems. Other systems can call the Customer MDM solution to get customer data. Thus, code in other systems was modified to disable cus tomer data management and to call out to Customer MDM instead. For those sys tems that could not be changed because they used packages solutions with no source code, the software was instructed to redirect all calls to this system for customer data to the Customer MDM. The worst-case scenario using this ap proach was that data would persist on these packaged legacy solutions, but it would no longer be used. This was another massive task, but the company be lieved that as long as the same customer data resided in two places, it would have data quality problems and spend more money fixing problems later on.

Phase 1 for the life insurance division was to manage new business (i.e., incom ing customer data for new life insurance policies). The new business system, un derwriting system, and the life policy administration system were modified to only deal with the Customer MDM solution for these new customers. No massive batch loads of existing customer data were needed, as this phase encompassed new business only. When the customer data comes in as a new business, the system checks whether this customer is already an existing customer in the policy administration system. If yes, it transfers whatever customer data it can get to the Customer MDM solution, using a continuous conversion approach. This data will be consolidated with incoming new data to get the most current version. The customer data in the policy administration system will be marked to indicate that it is now in the new Customer MDM solution, and any future process should ask for customer data from there.

It was decided to select new business for this phase because it allows customer data to come in one record at a time, gradually building up the Customer MDM solution. In this way, performance can be controlled. Also, from a business perspective, this provides immediate improvement to the underwriting areas of risk management, as the system can automatically determine preexisting customers and what other life insurance coverage is already in place.

A batch load of existing customer data for the life insurance business to the Customer MDM solution was done in Phase 2. During subsequent phases, customer data from other product lines were included.

Manufacturing

In our next case study, a manufacturing company had many business lines, referred to here as A, B, C, and D. Each product line is run autonomously and controls its own profit-and-loss outcomes and systems. One year, a new CEO came on board from a company that happens to be a customer for business lines A, C, and D, but also a vendor for business lines B and C. After a few weeks on the job, the new CEO wants to pay a visit to the CEO of his previous company, who is also a personal friend. This new CEO, before going to see his old buddy, wants to know how much business is accomplished between these two companies, so that he know where he stands when talking to his old buddy—that is, at the end of the day, is he giving him more business or the other way around? This will impact the way he discusses business and negotiates for better terms and conditions.

When the new CEO asked for a report showing how his new company is doing vis-à-vis his old one, it took weeks for all the IT shops to consolidate the data. He ended up with three different reports that show three different results.

These reports were not consistent and cannot be trusted, because the four operating units use different Enterprise Resource Planning (ERP) and finance systems. In addition, the CEO's old company has many subsidiaries and related companies whose relationships are not captured by some of these systems. So, there is no way to know how these companies are related to each other and to the manufacturing company in question, or how the net business is placed.

The CEO then tasked the small-enterprise IT unit, which is more involved in setting IT standards and best practices than in running an operational system, to provide a solution to this problem.

The enterprise IT head and his architects decided to design a solution using a Customer MDM hub to consolidate all customer data held in multiple disparate systems across all operating units. In addition, they needed to enhance the data, so that proper organizational hierarchies, relationships, and key stakeholders are readily identifiable, in order to be of value to the business and to produce a direct report for the CEO. The problem was that the enterprise IT doesn't control the operating line IT units and the systems that they run. Rather than getting the CEO to dictate that every operating unit IT had to cooperate and commit resources to this project, the enterprise IT head decided to use a different approach to win them over instead.

He decided to install and run the Customer MDM solution on his own unit and ask the four operating lines to contribute whatever up-to-date customer data they had. Typically, this customer data was found in extracts that the operating units performed from their ERP and financial systems to feed their own data warehouse. So, for Phase 1, the consolidation style approach was used to channel all this customer data in batch mode into the Customer MDM solution. The Customer MDM solution then performed the necessary cleansing, merging, and de-duplication. The Customer MDM solution technicians also subscribed to Dun & Bradstreet (D&B; an external customer data provider that provides enhanced data, including organizational hierarchies, key person data, etc.) to get supplementary data that the operating units did not have but might find useful. This D&B data was used to improve the matching and de-duplication process, and the organizational hierarchies and key person data were loaded to enhance internal customer data whenever possible.

A nice, easy-to-use graphical user interface accessible via the Internet was designed to front-end this Customer MDM solution. This user interface was then given freely to all users in all operating unit. Users could now search for all the key stakeholders for their customers, and for organizational hierarchies that might show other existing customers that they can sell to. In addition, the operating units can also find out whether their customers are actually vendors or customers of another operating unit. Using this information, units can compare notes and coordinate business.

Over time, word spread throughout the corporation about the new Customer MDM solution and its "golden" customer data. People across all operating lines started to sign on and use it. Whenever users found errors in the data, they notified enterprise IT. These activities were key to beginning the conversation between operating units and the Customer MDM unit that would lead to discovering why data was wrong or out of date. It became obvious very quickly that if the systems could communicate and integrate faster and better, some of these errors would go away.

Thus, over time, new IT projects were funded by operating units to help their own IT systems synchronize customer data with that of the enterprise Customer MDM IT unit. This is a nice consolidation-style approach that ultimately leads to a co-existence approach that makes the Customer MDM data more reliable. And it was a smart way to get individual operating units to see the value of a system with combined customer (and vendor) data.

~

After reviewing these case studies, you can see that there is more than one way to implement a Customer MDM solution in your organization. You can use different implementation styles and approaches (consolidation, registry, co-existence, transactional, batch ETL load, and continuous conversion) to help you get going. The key is to find a small enough project so that you can mix and match the various styles and approaches to deliver measurable business values and rapidly increase customer-centric data management for your business. The next chapter looks at the data governance issues that must be decided on before successfully undertaking a Customer MDM project.

Chapter 6

Data Governance

When considering the implementation of a Customer Master Data Management (MDM) solution in any organization, one has to tackle the issue of data governance. *Data governance* deals with the issues of data definition, data ownership, process rules for the data, usage of the data, and other aspects of data management. Data governance is essentially the organizational structures, processes, and tools needed to ensure each piece of data is properly handled for enterprise usage.

Data governance issues are not related to Customer MDM solutions only, but this type of project will bring these issues up very quickly. When customer data is managed at individual business unit silos without consideration for enterprise us age, each business unit is in full control of its customer data and can dictate its own rules and processes to use that data. But, when customer data comes to gether in an enterprise Customer MDM solution, to be shared and used by every business unit, problems start to arise if everyone doesn't agree on how usage of this data is to be governed.

Let's take the case of Robert Smith mentioned earlier, who has his address listed as 1 Main Street in the bank's Demand Deposit Account (DDA) system and 2 Main Street in the bank's credit card system. The core banking unit or savings & loans unit will look at Robert Smith's data and decide that 1 Main Street is the correct address. Similarly, the credit card unit would have no doubt that 2 Main Street is the correct address. There is no reason for either unit to think that the addresses they have for Robert may be bad. But, when Robert Smith's records come together in a new Customer MDM solution, to be consolidated in one place and used by all units, that Robert Smith has two different addresses suddenly be comes very apparent. As mentioned earlier, 1 Main Street could be correct, 2 Main Street could be correct, or both could be correct. The questions become which business unit is going to own which address, and who will investigate and resolve this conflict? Or, should a new enterprise unit be set up to own this prob lem and investigate and resolve it? (We are using an inconsistent address as an example, but it could just as well be other data elements like birth date, gender, IDs, etc.) These issues must be thought out *before* the Customer MDM solution is implemented. The governing structure to resolve these data issues, including tools to use, processes to follow, and organizational structures and committees to decide on ownership and rules, must be agreed upon and resolved up front. If not, the project will likely fail.

The data governance issues must be owned by both IT and business. The busi ness side of the equation must define the governing rules and processes; the IT side must provide the tools and systems to automate the processes, if this is at all possible.

I have seen some Customer MDM project driven purely from the IT side, with no business involvement. This is a recipe for disaster. The moment the system goes live, invariably data quality issues arise. When an address conflict arises, or, worse, when after a batch load of customer data over the weekend shows thou sands of duplicate suspects—who is going to resolve these issues? It has to be the business side of the equation that decides what data is correct, not the IT side. If unresolved, you might as well not have implemented the Customer MDM solu tion, as the data cannot be trusted and the business cannot use it.

There are exceptions to this, such as when you are implementing a Customer MDM using consolidation style, as in the manufacturing case described in the previous chapter. In this case, the data was not meant to affect operational sys tems during the early phase of implementation, so business input was not manda tory. In the manufacturing case study, the consolidation style primarily was used to allow all business units to see the value of an enterprise Customer MDM solu tion and to get all parties on board. Once you have all parties on board, however, and especially when they are from different units, you need to set up the neces sary data governance practices to ensure proper stewardship of your customer data as the various units begin to integrate with the Customer MDM solution.

An entire book could be written on data governance issues and best practices. But here we'll give a simplistic overview of this issue, so that you can appreciate its importance. In general, data governance falls into the following three areas:

- Governing structure and committee:
  - ➤ You need to set up committees or groups of people who are going to be involved in data governance. Generally, you will need at least two groups. The first is a senior-level governing council with representation from senior members of the various operating units. This senior committee will have to define the ownership of the data, and the rules and processes governing the management of data and resolution of data quality problems. The corporate policies regarding the creation, acquisition, management, and usage of data will have to be defined by this group.
  - ➤ The second group is the execution committee, and it consists of those people who will actually be executing the corporate data governance policy, as defined by the senior executive group. This group will follow the rules and processes defined, and will monitor compliance. They will report back to the senior committee on the status of compliance and consult with them on problem resolution.

- Governing process:
  - ➤ The governing process defined by the senior committee must be suitable to the business. Most organizations will implement a very centralized "command-and-control" type of process, in which a new enterprise data governance or data stewardship group is formed to resolve any data quality issues. This group is responsible for contacting individual operating units and sometime customers to resolve any data quality issues.
  - ➤ Another approach is a decentralized model, that has only a very small skeleton enterprise group to manage work flow and coordinate activities. The resolution of any data quality issues is pushed back down for the individual operating units to resolve. In the case of Robert Smith, the core banking or saving & loan unit will be notified of the potential conflicts, together with the credit card unit. Both units can work together to verify the addresses are correct, and they may call the customer to achieve that. They will then submit any changes (if needed) back to the Customer MDM solution.

- ➢ Detail processes would also have to be decided on other data issues, such as data privacy issues dealing with data sharing and marketing solicitation preferences across different business lines. Depending on industries, some of these issues may involve legal compliance implications, and the process should be properly addressed to ensure legal compliance.

- ▪ Tools:
  - ➢ Once the governing structure and processes are defined, IT can work on delivering tools to help in the smooth operation of these new processes. These may include the production of data quality reports and user interfaces to resolve duplicate data or to resolve data quality issues.
  - ➢ A meta-data tool might be introduced to govern the definition of each data item, including its ownership and usage, and to provide traceability on where the piece of data is and how it is connected to other data in various systems.
  - ➢ Work flow engines might be introduced to ensure that each data governance step is followed and tracked. Escalation procedures might be invoked if any exception in processing occurs.
  - ➢ To manage data security and privacy, specific tools may be introduced to define the possible roles and ownership profiles for each user and customer.
  - ➢ These are simply the tools that can help ensure the smooth operation of data governance structures, rules, and processes. There will be many other tools to think about once the Customer MDM solution project gets going.

Data governance is an important area for careful discussion and research before the implementation of Customer MDM solutions. Unless a clearly documented policy for how data is used and managed is in place, migrating data into the Customer MDM system can quickly deteriorate into a chaos of mismatched information, duplication of data and effort, conflict and competition among various business units, a lack of accountability for errors, and infringements of privacy and regulatory compliance rules.

Chapter 7

Be Careful What You Ask For: Your IT Might Actually Deliver

In the quest for a more customer-centric organization, many executives ask their IT divisions to deliver a Customer Relationship Management (CRM) system, a Single Customer View system, or a Client Master File system to help coordinate how the business deals with its customers. In response, some IT shops have delivered call center solutions, such as CRM systems that only provide (at best) some form of Single Customer View to call center representatives but not to other channels, like the web or sales units. Although CRM was originally intended as a broad strategy to improve customer service, unfortunately, over the last decade, some software vendors have narrowed the concept and terminology to suit their call center solution sets.

Other IT shops have implemented a Single Customer View solution using a data warehouse, which is typically used for analytical purposes with after-the-fact data (data that could have been input last night, last week, or some time in the past). Systems based on a Single Customer View will provide a narrow focus on the single customer, but use static, out-of-date data. You get to "view" the data but you cannot act on it. Even if you do, because the data is out-of-date, you can't be definitely sure that you are using the right data in its current state.

Still other IT shops went on to create Client Master File (typically called Client Information File or CIF) systems. But Client Master Files are simply databases; the logic needed to process the data resides in other systems. This causes data integrity issues and redundancy of business logic. For example, one system might validate an address one way and another system in a different way. This might cause data integrity issues in the future. Thus, in most cases, CIF implementation is only successful for one line of business (LOB). When it is implemented across multiple LOBs, the differing business logic used by various LOBs will cause data integrity issues; very soon, single LOBs will withdraw from the CIF implementation, convinced that it is designed only to benefit the first LOB that implemented it.

This is why Customer Master Data Management (MDM) solutions are so vital to the customer-centric organization. The key differentiator between Customer MDM solutions and CRM, data warehouse, and LOB-specific CIF is that Customer MDM is meant to be implemented and integrated in real-time to all touch-point systems, so that it can become the operational master of customer data. And although this may not be achieved during the initial phase of the project, it is definitely the desired objective in the long run.

Let's review again the case of Robert Smith, who has listed his address as 1 Main Street in the bank's Demand Deposit Account (DDA) system and as 2 Main Street in the credit card system. If a Customer MDM solution with real-time integration was in play for this situation, when 2 Main Street is entered during the credit card application, the Customer MDM solution would have detected the potential problem right away and sought resolution to confirm whether 1 Main Street, 2 Main Street, or both addresses were correct. In a traditional CRM, data warehouse, or LOB CIF implementation, the 2 Main Street address from the credit card application would come in too late, maybe even after business hours. As a result, these systems would have detected the symptom of the problem "after the fact," instead of resolving the potential data quality issue at the root cause, when the data was initiated. Although many people have the misconception that CRM, data warehouses, and LOB CIF will fix this type of data quality problem, in reality, these systems only fix the symptom of the problem (the wrong address), not the cause (that two different addresses were entered in two different systems).

One good way to test whether the CRM, data warehouse, or LOB CIF is helping to resolve this type of data quality issue is to imagine a customer buying multiple products from different LOBs at the same time. How many times must he enter the same information? Let's take our banking example again. Assume a customer enters a bank and wants to open a savings account, apply for a credit card, and open a stock trading account. A bank with a properly implemented Customer MDM solution would need the customer's common data, like name and address, entered only once, as this data can be shared by all LOB applications. This immediately eliminates a lot of data quality prob lems. A bank without a Customer MDM solution, but one that has CRM, data warehouse, and LOB CIF, would probably need the customer's common data entered three times to three different LOB applications (core banking, credit card, and trading). The CRM, data warehouse, and LOB CIF might ultimately catch any data quality issues that arise, but this would be "after the fact"—too late.

Management must understand many important concepts before requesting a Customer MDM solution. Some of these concepts are covered in the following sections.

Party vs. Customer

The Party concept is one of the most fundamental concepts in a flexible Cus tomer MDM solution. *Party* is a data model design construct that refers to any person or organization. Therefore, Party is not only your customer, but can also be your prospects, employees, producers, business partners, and others. For ex ample, I could be a bank teller (an employee) and also a customer of my bank (I have accounts in my bank). A good Customer MDM system should be able to know that there might be special processes that I might have to go through when I am processing my own account. Or, the system might stop me from processing my own account according to the bank's rules. Whether I am a cus tomer or an employee, I am the same person. So, the Customer MDM system should recognize me as such. Being a customer, employee, prospect, and/or business partner is just different roles that I assume, depending on the business process.

The Party construct is used by many leading IT organizations in their Customer MDM, CRM, and data warehouse solution designs. It's not a new idea, but it's important for flexibility. (Most IT vendors don't use the word Party, and in stead use the word *Customer* because it is easier to comprehend and sell.)

View vs. Operational

Another common requirement is for a system to provide a Single Customer View that allows a customer's data to be seen in a clean, single state (instead of duplicate). The ability to process in a clean single state, have up-to-date data, support operation processes, and support addition and changes is a requirement often implied by the business executive but often not understood by the IT shop. It's a matter of defining what exactly the solution should do. Many IT shops develop data warehouses to provide a Single Customer View to the business, but for business process users, the analytic capabilities of the data warehouse fall short of the customer-centric processes that they have in mind. Therefore, it is important to ask for real-time operation capabilities in Single Customer View systems.

Batch vs. Real-time

Back in the 1960s and 1970s, a lot of systems were designed to batch process data. Nowadays, however, most companies want real-time enabled systems for all business processes. In this competitive world, every single second is important. Therefore, every single second of up-to-date customer information is important if you are to be competitive. Unfortunately, many processes are still performed in batch mode. Processing a new credit card application is a good example. Although many banks accept online credit card applications, lots of them still have back-room operations to process and approve each application and submit the lots of successful and unsuccessful applications in batch to the appropriate systems for further processing. In addition, some business processes are time-based and naturally batch-driven processes, for example, identifying people who reach retirement age (many customers in a bank will have the same birth date) and monthly billing processes (since there is a maximum of 31 days in a month, each day, many customers will need to be billed). Therefore, a good Customer MDM solution has to handle both real-time and batch processes equally well.

Making It Proactive

When you have the chance to implement a new Customer MDM solution, take the opportunity to make sure the system is not just a passive one that accepts customer processing requests from other systems. If this system holds the "golden" copy of customer data, you can do a lot with the information in it, such as set up proactive customer management processes that originate from the Customer MDM system. For example, the system should be able to monitor for events and send out notifications to users on other systems to act. A bank for example, might want to configure the Customer MDM solution to monitor birth dates, so that shortly before a person reaches retirement age, the system can notify financial advisors to call the customer proactively and sell her financial products suitable for retirees. If they don't, the customer may soon be courted by another bank that has taken the initiative to sell her something appropriate for this moment in her life. Another example occurs when a customer calls to change her address. The Customer MDM system should send a notification to other systems that still hold the old address or to users who need to act based on an address change. For example, in a bank, when a customer calls to change the address for a savings account, this might affect an existing mortgage or home insurance account. Therefore, the appropriate LOB should be notified (if allowed by privacy legislation).

CRM and Data Warehouse: Are They the Customer-Centric Solution?

Many organizations in the past decade have tried to provide solutions to enable customer-centric management via CRM and data warehouse solutions. Most CRM solutions are designed to provide automation for specific channels, such as call centers and the sales force. They provide excellent user interfaces and workflows to automate the business processes of servicing and selling. But can they be the solution for providing customer-centric information and supporting customer-centric processes throughout the enterprise?

Data warehouses have also been successfully deployed in many organizations to collect, store, and analyze customer data across the enterprise. Successful organizations have used data warehouses to determine all kinds of metrics to measure a customer. Various business intelligence techniques are used to probe and mine the customer data to produce scores such as Life-Time Value, Propensity to Buy Certain Product, Propensity to Drop Certain Product, and the like. But can they be the solution for providing customer-centric information and supporting customer-centric processes throughout the enterprise?

Advantages and Misconceptions of the CRM Solution

Currently, major CRM solutions are mainly designed for specific channel auto
mation, such as handling of calls coming into a call center or assisting a sales
person to sell products. In call center CRM packages, features could include the
automatic detection of phone numbers (using computer-to-telephony technol
ogy), searching and displaying client data, screen pop-ups to prompt call center
associates on what to say, workflow to automatically trigger the next tasks, and
more. In sales force automation CRM packages, features could include the enter
ing of prospect/customer data, the display of multiple product options for the cus
tomer, order taking, and the like. Most CRM packages, but not all, have a
database to store information on the customer, product, and transaction, in order
to support the automation of their intended processes.

The advantages of these CRM packages are that they do provide best-of-breed
user interfaces and workflow to automate the services or sales aspects that they
are designed to automate. These packages provide an invaluable tool for many
call centers and sales forces.

Recently, CRM package vendors have been trying to position their database to be
the customer master that can be used across other systems in the enterprise. In re
ality, databases in the CRM packages cannot be the customer master for the fol
lowing reasons:

- CRM packages are typically LOB focused; therefore, the database
  modeling is typically LOB-specific as well and does not have the
  flexibility to be changed to handle other businesses.

- Most CRM packages have tightly coupled the database layer with the
  processing layer. Therefore, any changes to the database layer will have a
  ripple effect on changes to the processing layer as well, thus making
  changes very problematic and costly.

- Even for small organizations with only one CRM package, the system is
  only solving "after-the-fact" data, not detecting the root of the data quality
  problem.

Advantage and Misconceptions
of the Data Warehouse Solution

Many organizations have used a data warehouse to consolidate disparate data across the enterprise, to provide analytical capabilities. Typically, a data ware house is designed to load data in batch rather than be operational in real-time mode. Data is staged and loaded from source systems in durations that are typi cally controlled by these source systems. The loads could be hourly, daily, weekly, or monthly. The data modeling constructs are also fine-tuned for analytical purposes.

While loading customer data to the data warehouse, some organizations try to improve the quality of the customer data by cleansing it while loading. These cleansing activities could include name and address standardization and even some form of automated matching and de-duplication. But, these activities are one-way processes that must be repeated for every load. Unless the data ware house data is wiped out and reloaded, some of the matching and de-duplicated re sults already in the data warehouse may not be used for subsequent loads, therefore creating inconsistency and suspect quality.

A data warehouse might be able to provide some level of cleansed customer data and an initial attempt at unified customer view, but due to its batch-driven and analytical design, it can never be an operational system. Therefore, at best, the data warehouse provides a "view," but it is not good enough to be operational in real-time and be the true master. It will only solve "after-the-fact" data problems, not detect the source of the problems.

Some data warehouse vendors are introducing the concept of an active or dy namic warehouse that allows more real-time operation, but at heart, the data warehouse remains an analytical engine. It is perfectly acceptable that the ware house can make the end result of its analytics available in real-time (i.e., operationalizing the analytical results). After all, the data warehouse is the source and master of these analytical results. But, if the argument holds that the data warehouse can be made "active," to act as the customer master for common cus tomer data, then why stop at that? Since it has operational domain data other than customer data, then we should also be able to design the active data warehouse to replace the product, order, billing, CRM, Enterprise Resource Planning (ERP), and all other systems. Following this logic, all you would need in any organization is one massive active data warehouse to run your business—a proposition that does not make sense.

Can Existing Client File Deliver? Five Tests

Some organizations, especially larger ones with enough IT staff to be able to afford to build systems, have created CIF systems. This is especially common in banks, and, to a lesser extent, in insurance companies. Some banks have built CIFs since the 1970s, using older mainframe and database technologies such as COBOL, VSAM (flat) files, IMS (hierarchical-based) databases, IDMS (network-based) databases, and the like. Newer ones, built in the late 1980s and 1990s, use newer relational DBMS.

From my experiences, most home-grown CIFs have out-grown their original purpose. When they were built using the criteria of the moment, many of these CIFs were very good and served their purposes well. But with the changing world, especially with consolidation, resource sharing, and merger and acquisition activities, a lot of these CIFs are no longer flexible enough to meet requirements, nor do they have the speed demanded by their organizations to respond to change. In my experience, only a handful of companies have well-designed CIFs flexible enough to meet their organizational demands for many more years. The majority of those in use now will need major rework or need to be replaced. The following are five tests I make to find out how healthy a current CIF really is:

First Test: Is It Loosely Coupled?

You want your CIF to be loosely coupled, so that it can be called by and integrated with any system. Also, any future changes to the CIF, such as adding new data elements or new subject areas, will be easier since a loosely coupled system will not greatly affect calling systems.

Many CIFs that I see are not designed this way. For example, in many banks, the CIF is tightly coupled with one of the core banking systems. In a retail bank, this is typically the DDA system that handles the savings and checking accounts. Customer data from other systems, such as credit cards, loans, trading, etc., is loaded into the CIF in batch mode, as the real-time entries are tied to DDA functions. Any additional changes that are required by other product systems for their customers are typically treated as "second-class," as DDA functions dictate how customer data will be treated. Therefore, many times, the quality of the customer

data in this CIF is less than desirable, as it cannot be used by other product sys
tems in real time. Customer data from other systems is treated "after-the-fact."

Second Test: Is It Specific to a Line of Business?

Many CIFs that I see are built for the purpose of one LOB. Using our bank exam
ple again, many bank CIFs are built for retail customers. Therefore, they are not
used by the commercial or corporate LOBs, because they cannot handle the com
plexity of organizational hierarchies that are required for commercial or corpo
rate customers. In response, some banks have developed separate CIFs to handle
commercial or corporate clients.

When a bank has two CIFs, one for retail and one for commercial/corporate,
there will be fundamental problems in achieving a unified view of a customer.
For example, a retail customer may not have a lot of money deposited in the re
tail bank office, but this same customer could be a CEO of a major corporation
that is doing business with the bank's commercial site.

Third Test: Is It Based on Relational DBMS?

Although some organizations developed early CIFs using nonrelational DBMS
such as VSAM file, IMS databases, and IDMS databases, modern organizations
use relational DBMS because of the flexibility of the relational structure in al
lowing changes and dynamic joins to resolve complex relationships. A modern
CIF will definitely need to leverage all the capabilities afforded by relational
DBMS versus other file or database structures.

(In the past 15 years, I have not seen any new CIFs built using nonrelational data
base structures; that in itself should show the pitfalls of using older database
technologies.)

Fourth Test: Is It Party-based?

Although most modern CIF systems use relational DBMS (a big step forward in
terms of flexibility), most of the modeling concepts in these CIFs still use the old
paradigm of modeling a customer as "customer" instead of as a person or an or
ganization—the concept of a Party.

Every time I see a CIF data model with a table called "Customer" or "Client," my next questions are, "What if the customer is also an Employee or a Business Part ner? Would I see separate tables called 'Employee' and 'Business Partner'?" Well, if I do, then wouldn't the customer who is an employee or business partner now have her data in more than one place?

This same argument can be applied to any different roles that a customer may hold. Using our bank example again, what if the customer is a beneficiary of a trust, a financial advisor for another customer, or a prospect? Would this same person who plays different roles have his information in many different role-based tables?

The mistake of creating role-based tables named "Customer," "Prospect," "Bene ficiary," "Trustee," "Employee," etc. is very common. This ultimately forces a person's or organization's data to be stored in many places, thus breaking the law of having one single instance of master data, and thus leading to data quality issues.

A well-tested, flexible design treats each customer as a Party. By definition, party can be a person or an organization. Whether this party is a customer, prospect, beneficiary, trustee, or employee, these actually are merely roles that the party plays in his lifecycle of dealing with your organization, and they should be mod eled using a separate "Role" or "Relationship" table. Most party-based models typically use the "Role" table to manage product-related roles. For example, as "customer" of an account, "beneficiary" of an insurance policy, "trustee" of a trust, and the like. The "Relationship" table is typically used to manage inter-party relationships, such as "employee" of a company, "child" of a parent, or "business partner" among two parties.

The Party-based relational modeling concept is not new; it's been around for about 20 years and is widely used by major database and application vendors.

Fifth Test: Is It Real-time?

I debated whether to include this last test. It seems so obvious a requirement that it shouldn't be thought of as a test. But I've been in situations where I discuss with a client a current CIF system for hours (or even days) without realizing that the CIF in question is only available to accept data in batch mode. Or, alterna tively, it can support real-time for the host system that it is coupled with—like the core banking system—but other systems have to send in their customer data in batch. Therefore, customer data from other systems gets "after-the-fact" treatment and the data quality cannot be trusted.

This is a real-time world that we live in. If an organization uses a batch-driven CIF and still thinks it can be competitive, then this organization doesn't need to be worrying about customer-centricity. And the content in this book will be of no use.

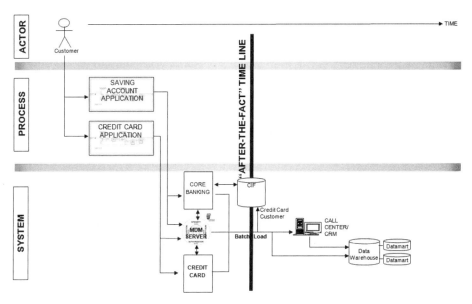

Figure 7.1: The Customer MDM solution detects and resolves data problems at source, in real-time, not "after-the-fact"

The line-of-visibility diagram in Figure 7.1 depicts how a Customer MDM solution differs from CIF, call center/CRM, and data warehouse solutions in resolving data quality problems. As soon as a customer opens a savings account, his customer data goes into the Customer MDM solution. It might also end up in the core banking CIF. Now, assume this same customer opens a credit card account at the same time. The data will again immediately be sent to the MDM Server solution. At that point, any data quality issues will be detected and hopefully resolved by the Customer MDM solution on the spot, while the customer is still there. The CIF, on the other hand, might get its data from the credit card system (or MDM system) in batch overnight or "too late." It has crossed the "after-the-fact" timeline, and any detection and resolution after this time is only solving the "symptom" of the data quality problem, rather than resolving it at source. The call center/CRM solution typically gets its customer data even later, again in batch mode. The data warehouse gets its data later still. Both of these systems have data that crosses the "after-the-fact" line as well, solving the symptom rather than root cause.

I have seen companies that spend years and lots of money making their CIF, call center/CRM, or data warehouse into their Customer MDM solution. At completion, these solutions still require a customer to fill in and enter the same data multiple times when he purchases multiple products at once, because there is no sharing of common data at source. These multiple copies of the same data will eventually end up going to the CIF, call center/CRM, or data warehouse solution in batch mode, and any data quality problems will be detected then. Many of these companies don't realize that these solutions are not resolving the problem. They are just resolving the symptoms of the problem "after-the-fact."

Chapter 8

Other Master Data Management Data Domains

This book has concentrated on Customer (or Party) domains within master data, but other important data domains are also considered master data, especially Product and Location. The most obvious one is the Product data domain. Many companies start their Customer Master Data Management (MDM) journey through implementing MDM for Product data. For example, these Product MDM implementations are very typical for manufacturing, retail, and distribution companies, to help with processes that create a new product, perform item management of products, manage product catalogs, and enable product data for e-commerce. Banks and insurance companies are also using the Product domain to keep track of the master product catalog listing of the products they can sell to a customer.

Another master data domain is Location. Real-time access to the Location domain is becoming more important with the increased proliferation of smart phones with Global Positioning Service (GPS) devices. For example, a property and casualty insurance company can use the Location domain to differentiate service to their customers. When one of their customers has a car accident and calls into the insurance company for assistance, the system can detect the location that this person is calling from. Upon positive identification of the caller and review of the coverage and benefits of her car insurance, the insurance company might realize that she is eligible for free towing service to the nearest authorized garage. The location obtained from

- 83 -

the GPS device can act as the location token to search through the MDM solution for possible tow trucks and authorized garages nearest to this customer at that par ticular time. This type of automated service saves time and increases customer sat isfaction, and it can be used as a great insurance product differentiator. Other industries, such as retail and manufacturing, have used Location extensively to identify and manage the locations of their goods and suppliers.

The primary master data domains are Party, Product, and Location. The Account domain is important because it ties these three data domains together (Fig. 8.1). For example, a person (Party domain) might go to a bank branch (another Party do main) at a certain street address (Location domain). While there, he might look at all the products/services (Product domain) offered by this bank at this branch. He might be interested in the term deposit savings product. So, with the help of a teller, he can open a term deposit savings account that spells out the terms and conditions of this product and the ownership of this account (i.e., the person). Therefore, this account doesn't exist until you combine this person with this product at this loca tion. Mastering of the Account domain is performed by default when you start to master at least the Party domain and the Product domain. You can also further ex tend the usage of this master account by providing account bundling and instantiating special terms and conditions for these combined accounts.

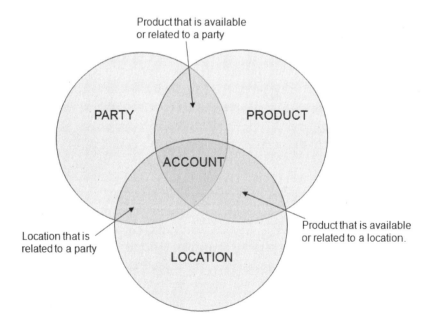

Figure 8.1: Multiple MDM data domains: Party, Product, Location, and Account

ome early adopters of MDM solutions have started to look into mastering all
ese MDM data domains in their organization, regardless of whether they started
om the Customer domain, Product domain, or Location domain, thus beginning
e implementation of a multiple-domain MDM.

Conclusion

e era of the "customer-centric" organization is upon us, with its promise of
st, efficient, and worry-free interactions between business and customers. The
ustomer MDM solution provides a first step toward the successful implementa
n of such an ideal. In this book, we've discussed how customers are defined,
at their needs are, and how customer needs and business process needs can be
egrated, using a single, master data repository that allows real-time processing
d that can provide all branches of a business with relevant and timely customer
ormation.

the concepts of master data management evolve and mature, businesses will
d more applications that lend themselves to this solution. From marketing and
s to service, in the quest for a truly customer-centric organization, the Cus-
er MDM solution will return big dividends in improved efficiency and re-
ed waste.